Flash

Cooking

Flash

Cooking

Fit Fast Flavours
for Busy People
Laura Santtini

Photography by Adam Laycock

Quadrille
PUBLISHING

_____
This book is for you

WWW.LAURASANTTINI.COM

Contents

Flash Defined

Flash 1 *verb* Shine or cause to shine with a bright but brief or intermittent light. 2 *verb informal* Display conspicuously so as to impress. 3 *verb informal* Show one's genitals in public.

Flash Cooking 1 *verb* Shine or cause to shine with bright but quickly prepared HEALTHFUL dishes. 2 *verb informal* Display conspicuous culinary skills so as to impress 3 *verb informal* Show one's culinary genius in public.

Flash Flavour 1 *verb* Shine or cause to shine with an artfully crafted flavour bomb, explosions of flavour causing bright bursts of de-light. 2 *verb informal* Conspicuously combine flavours so as to impress 3 *verb informal* Show one's garam masala in public.

Flash Fit 1 *verb* Shine or cause to shine with bright HEALTHFUL energy, inner light and self-love. 2 *verb informal* Display conspicuous confidence so as to impress 3 *verb informal* Show one's privates in private.

What is Flash cooking?

Laura Santtini

Flash cooking is all about fast, healthful, easy-to-prepare, nutritious, flavour-packed meals that look great, taste extraordinary and promote wellbeing. Moreover, this book is about helping readers develop the confidence to pair unusual and perhaps new flavourings with their usual basic main ingredients. It will give you a passport to the flavours of all the continents, so you can confidently cross borders and create your own world of deliciousness. Flash cooking is about developing the confidence to add a splash of soy sauce to a Bolognese, or mango chutney and Worcestershire sauce to a traditional vinaigrette dressing. Quickly prepared ingredients and fast flavours literally flash in the pan, transforming everyday ingredients into tasty healthy meals that will also help keep you trim and fit.

Flash Cooking is the future for everyday cooking – a brand-new fusion of 'scratch' cooking and health food. As we become more time-, health- and figure-conscious, cooking that is more complex and high in calories will be reserved for weekends, special occasions, relaxation therapy, high days and holidays.

For a fit, healthful life, I suggest that the ideal ratio of Flash cooking to non-Flash cooking should be 80/20. For example, cook Flash Monday to Friday, then at the weekends enjoy whatever you fancy. Having read Michael Pollan's inspirational *New York Times* best-seller, *The Food Rules,* I now make a point of cooking from scratch any indulgences I fancy at the weekend (unless we are going out). You will be surprised how much more delicious a gooey pudding tastes when you have taken the time to make it yourself. In his book, Pollan reminds us that this is exactly how special treats are supposed to be consumed, because of the effort and time taken to prepare them, highlighting that the mass-manufacture of foods has meant that we are now able to consume high-calorie 'treat' food at any time on any day. Flash cooking is all about putting those treats back where they belong, and filling the week with satisfying fit flavours to transform your life in a truly positive way.

'Food is our common ground, a universal experience.' *James Beard*

In the spirit of this quote and in the knowledge that nature holds many a remedy in her unfathomable magnificence, I have travelled the world with my taste buds and combined nature's natural remedies with everyday ingredients to create easy, tasty, healthful meals. Flash Cooking was born from a culinary journey where I lost old habits, acquired new customs and found a new version of myself.

Today we are looking inwards even more and sustainability is no longer limited only to fishing and farming but to our own bodily resources. As we sow seeds of doubt regarding irresponsible farming and food policy, we are also questioning our own conspicuous consumption (continued on page 9)

The Flash Philosophy

'Eat food, not too much, mostly plants.' *Michael Pollan*

Essential, do-able and intellectually delicious, follow Pollan's simple mantra to promote wellbeing at your table and within your personal temple.

Eat food, not too much: stick to proper mealtimes and reasonable portions. I have a 'no second helping' rule and generally do not snack between meals.

Mostly plants: protein is vital to healthy living and muscle maintenance, but we do not need too much. Make sure that the protein on your plate is no bigger than a deck of cards or i-phone and that the rest is plant matter.

In addition, it is important to: Drink plenty of water: a minimum of 8 glasses a day for adults. Take regular exercise: stretch and move your body and get things going on a daily basis. It can even just be touching your toes. This is not necessarily about strenuous gym work, but simply, say, a brisk walk or a yoga class or even just a simple quick stretch. The important thing is to build up some heat from within and feel the glow as it pumps your blood around your body, carrying all the goodness you have been eating, and expelling what is surplus through your pores. Regular exercise can keep all sorts of things away, from depression to bone disease.

Flash Plate

Make sure that the protein on your plate is no bigger than a deck of cards or i-phone and that the rest is mostly plants. In Flash Cooking 'mostly plants' = leafy green veg + salad or low-GI veg to include plenty of broccoli. Low-GI (Glycaemic Index) foods are digested by the body more slowly, keeping you feeling full for longer and giving you their energy over a longer period of time).

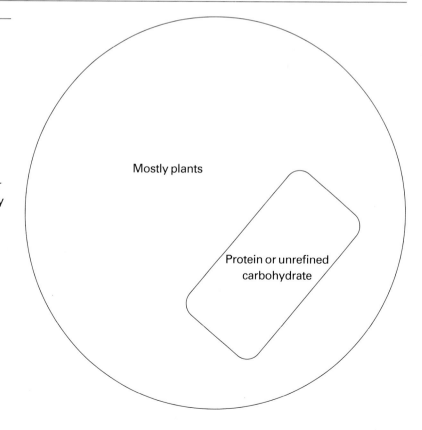

Mostly plants

Protein or unrefined carbohydrate

Moderation in all Things

We now have made in one design
The Utile and Dulce join,
And taught the poor and men of
wealth
To reconcile their tastes to health.
Restrain each forward appetite
To dine with prudence and delight,
And, careful all our rules to follow,
To masticate before they swallow.
'Tis thus Hygeia guides our pen
To warn the greedy sons of men
To moderate their wine and meat
And eat to live, not live to eat.

*Apicius Redivivus or the Cook's
Oracle* Dr William Kitchiner (1817)

of food, with loaded questions like how much longer can my body 'sustain' my eating and drinking irresponsibly without irrevocably damaging my long-term health… how can I reap the benefits of a new and nutritious way of life?

It would appear that with the advancement of medical science and the availability of information, that in the enlightened age of Aquarius we care more about living longer healthful lives in good-looking healthful bodies that ever before. So responsible eating goes hand in hand with responsible farming, especially in a world where the female eunuch has been buried alongside the dodo. 'Yummy' is the new middle-aged mummy, and MILF the new menopause.

It has also become quite clear that fat is certainly no longer a feminist issue, and has even become a huge problem for our children. You only have to look at the media to see that the quest for good health and eternal youth is now completely unisex. Men's magazines and targeted advertisements demonstrate that men are also working out to stay fit, watching what they eat and spraying themselves with products that claim to make them irresistible. Children too are looking to us for a good example on how to cook and eat. It is important that they learn the right things early on in life, so they don't have to make major adjustments or battle with food issues later on – especially as the U-turn on eating is a notoriously difficult manoeuvre.

Our personal eating pathway is usually built as we are growing up. When a choice is made to 'unlearn' that which is not healthy – be that in mind or body – it is necessary to build a new pathway forward. In the early days, this is little more than a dusty track, so it is very easy to return to the main road of bad habits. So, until you are sure that your new and sturdy pathway has been built, you have to be very vigilant. That said, you will know if you have built a new path to healthy eating when something throws you into a wobble, but you nonetheless manage to stay on course rather than reach for the cake. Children who build a positive eating pathway from a young age will not have to relearn eating behaviour, as this will be their true path and should help them make healthy choices down the line. Good body image is key to self-confidence and I believe that confidence is one of the greatest gifts we can give our children. For Flash children see page 163.

At a recent talk in New York, Michael Pollan suggested individuals or families create a simple personal eating policy for themselves as a general guide. "Use simple statements that are achievable within a balanced life, it might just be as simple as 'I/we do not buy cereal that changes the colour of the milk'".

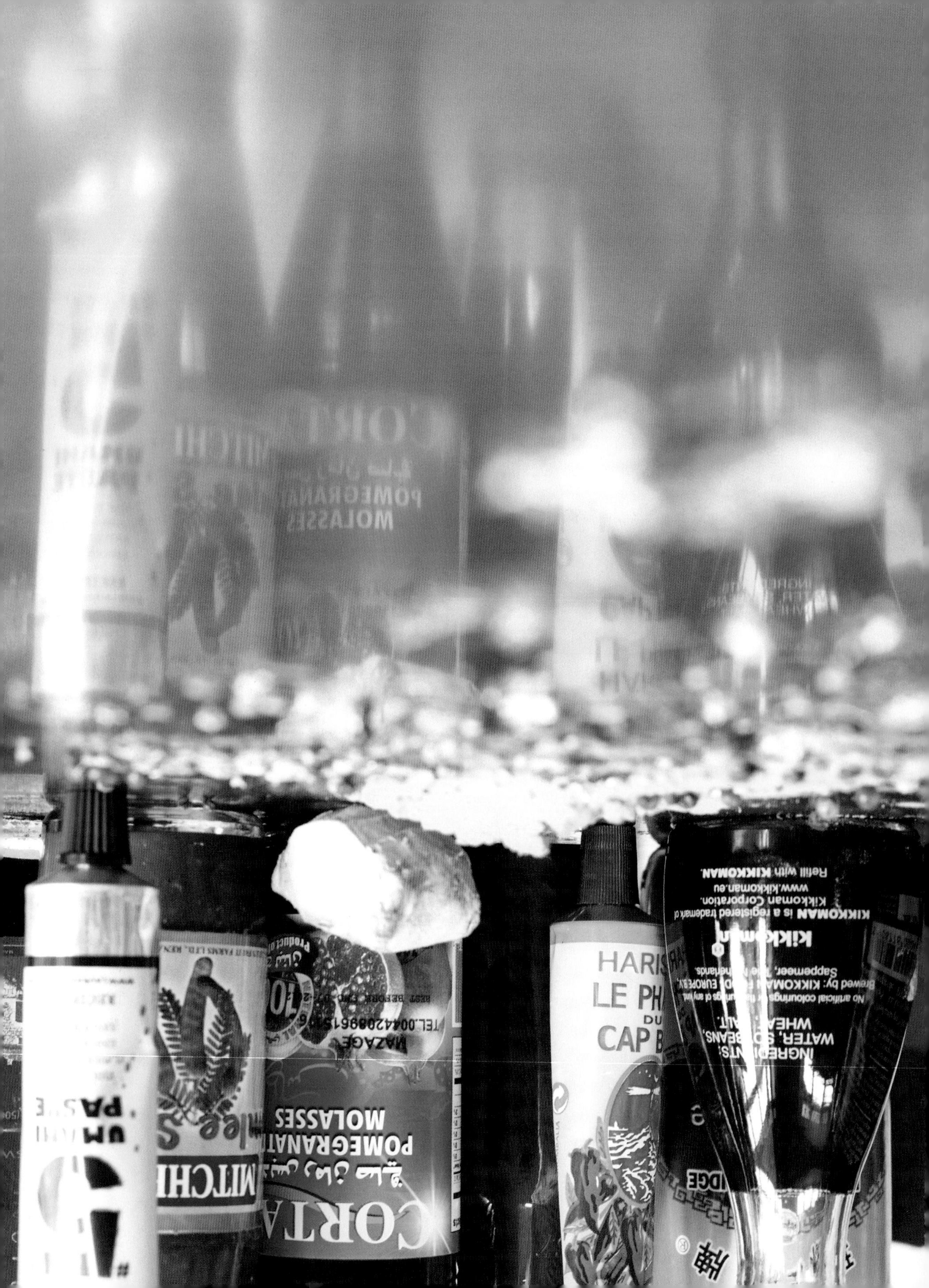
HARIS
LE PH
DU
CAP B

Flash

Flavours

This chapter shows you how easy it is to access flavour quickly by means of world flavour bombs designed to give you delicious and immediate flavouring mixes at your fingertips – and the confidence to globe-trot your everyday cooking to another level.

The idea is to enjoy making several blends in advance in the knowledge that you will sizzle with Flash style once you have them. If you need to take shortcuts, though, no problem: you can still Flash with flavour using the simple and accessible commercial versions I have also indicated. Tongue travellers and palate passengers fasten your seat belts – the journey starts here.

Unless otherwise indicated, all the flavouring recipes in this chapter make enough for today with plenty left for tomorrow. These traditional seasoning blends can also be bought ready-made in most good supermarkets and spice shops.

Seasonings

To get the best from these flavourings, whenever possible use whole spices (not herbs, of course) and lightly toast them over a low heat in a dry pan until fragrant. When completely cool, use a small coffee grinder or spice mill to blend them to a fine powder (no need for this in the case of the Herbes de Provence).

Combine all the ingredients until well blended.

Sprinkle over fish, meat, etc., before cooking them.

Store in an airtight container, as once ground, they will start to lose their flavour after a time.

Flash Substitutes: commercial versions of these traditional seasoning blends can be bought in most good supermarkets and spice shops, or ordered on the net.

Western
Herbes de Provence

(This does not need to be ground!)

- 2 tbsp dried rosemary
- 1 tbsp dried oregano
- 1 tbsp dried thyme
- 1 tbsp dried savory
- 1 tbsp dried tarragon

Middle Eastern
Baharat

- 2 tbsp ground black pepper
- 1½ tbsp ground cumin
- 1 tbsp ground coriander
- 1 tbsp ground cinnamon
- 1 tbsp ground cloves
- ½ tsp ground cardamom
- 2 tsp smoked paprika (unsmoked will do)
- 2 tsp ground nutmeg

Indian
Garam Masala

If you can't find cardamom seeds, use the pods and shell them yourself to get at the black seeds inside. To break up whole nutmegs, wrap them in a cloth and bash them with a rolling pin.

- 2 tbsp cardamom seeds
- 1½ cinnamon sticks (about 10-15cm/ 4-6 inches in total)
- 2 tsp black cumin (ordinary will do)
- 2 tsp whole cloves
- 2 tsp black peppercorns
- 1 tsp fennel seeds
- ½ nutmeg
- 2 bay leaves

Far Eastern
Five-spice Powder

- 3 star anise
- 2 medium cinnamon sticks (about 15-20cm/6-8 inches in total)
- 3 tbsp Sichuan peppercorns
- 2 tbsp fennel seeds
- ½ tsp whole cloves

Glazes

Mix 1 tablespoon of olive oil with the following and brush all over meat or fish before cooking, to give both colour and flavour.

Flash Umami

Umami = savoury deliciousness, the scientifically proven fifth taste (over and above sweetness, bitterness, sourness and saltiness).

You can literally double your deliciousness by adding ingredients naturally high in umami to your cooking. As a devotee to deliciousness, I set about creating Taste #5 Umami Paste, the worlds first umami paste, an essential and affordable scratch cooking tool designed to make good cooks great cooks and great cooks extraordinary cooks. I am so grateful that the demand for this simple idea has been such that my paste is now available in shops all over the world, with umami fans requesting further recipe ideas daily. For this reason I have therefore included Taste #5 Umami Paste in this book alongside plenty of equally delicious everyday alternatives, from the iconic Worcestershire sauce, to Parmesan cheese, soy sauce and the humble anchovy. I hope this will be useful to all those who have asked and not an obligation for those who have not. For further information on umami, see www.umamiinfo.com.

Western
Balsamic Glaze

- 1 tsp green or red pesto
- 2 tsp thick balsamic vinegar
- sea salt and freshly ground black pepper to taste

Middle Eastern
Pomegranate Glaze

- 1/2 tsp rose (or ordinary) harissa paste or powder
- 1 tsp pomegranate molasses
- sea salt to taste

Indian
Tamarind Glaze

- 1 tsp tamarind paste
- 1/2 tsp medium curry paste
- sea salt and freshly ground black pepper to taste

Far Eastern
Soy Glaze

- 1 tsp soy sauce
- 1 tsp mirin
- runny honey to taste

Umami
Taste #5 Umami Paste Glaze

- 1 tsp Taste #5 Umami Paste
- freshly ground black pepper to taste

Rubinades

As the name suggests, 'rubinades' are a flavour-packed cross between a rub and a marinade. Once you get the hang of them you will ask yourself how you ever lived without them.

Whiz up these simple recipes and use them to transform your barbecues, Sunday roasts and grills. You can use them to flavour meat, poultry or fish, and they act as a seasoning, marinade and wonderful basting tool.

For roasting, make sure that you baste your meat regularly with a splash of wine or stock – or both – so as not to burn the rubinade ingredients. You will delight in the gravy that collects in the pan.

I have given you five basic recipes, but once you've got the hang of the idea I am sure you will enjoy experimenting.

For these quick flavour boosters, place all ingredients except the salt and pepper in a food processor with a little olive oil and pulse until chopped – not to a pulp but into little pieces as opposite. Add more oil to make a runny paste, season with salt and pepper. Rub the mix over the meat or fish. These recipes yield enough for a whole butterfly of lamb (which is wonderful) or 6 chicken pieces, with enough in the fridge for another meal.

Note: don't eat any of the mixtures raw after the meat etc. has been in it.

Western
Rosemary and Sage Rubinade

For an umami kick, add a good squeeze of Taste #5 Umami Paste and a teaspoon of sweet or smoked paprika.

- 1 onion, quartered
- bunch of rosemary, leaves only
- bunch of sage, leaves only
- 3 garlic cloves
- sea salt and freshly ground black pepper
- olive oil

Middle Eastern
Mint, Lemon and Harissa Rubinade

- 1 red onion, quartered
- bunch of mint
- 2 small preserved lemons
- 1 heaped tsp harissa paste or powder (rose or ordinary)
- 3 garlic cloves
- sea salt and freshly ground black pepper
- olive oil

Indian
Curry and Coriander Rubinade

For a little sweet with your sour, try adding some mango chutney or lime pickle to taste.

- 1 onion, quartered
- bunch of coriander
- 1 tbsp imli or tamarind paste
- 1-2 tsp medium curry paste
- 3 garlic cloves
- 1 green chilli (deseeded for less heat)
- squeeze of lime juice
- sea salt and freshly ground black pepper
- olive oil

Far Eastern
Ginger and Chilli Rubinade

Note: I have used maple syrup instead of honey because it does not burn so readily.

- 1 onion, quartered
- 1 bunch of spring onions
- 1 red chilli pepper (deseeded for less heat)
- 3 garlic cloves
- 5cm/2-inch piece of fresh ginger root
- 3 tbsp soy sauce
- dash of nam pla fish sauce
- 1-3 tbsp maple syrup (optional, depending on whether or not you want some sweetness)
- sea salt and freshly ground black pepper
- sesame oil

Pastes

Apart from the Far Eastern Sweet Satay Paste, to make these simply mix all the ingredients, ideally using a hand blender. The pastes can be used raw or cooked.

Combine them with mayonnaise and live Greek-style yogurt for differently flavoured Ma-Yo crusts (see page 38). Use them as they are to stuff fillets or add a little olive oil to create tasty seasoning glazes for meat, chicken or fish. Create new Finishing Yogurts (see page 21) or simply use to garnish soups, run through wheat-free pasta, noodles, or to add flavour and colour when rehydrating couscous.

Covered with a thin layer of olive oil, these pastes will keep in the fridge for up to a week.

Western
Artichoke and Caper Paste

Flash Substitute:
green or red pesto

- 250g artichokes in oil, drained
- 1 tbsp capers, drained
- 1 tbsp tapenade (black olive paste)
- 2 garlic cloves
- juice of 1/2 lemon
- handful of fresh basil leaves
- freshly ground black pepper

Middle Eastern
Red Pepper and Orange Paste

Flash Substitute: bought harissa paste (mix with some sun-dried tomato paste for less chilli heat).

- 200g bottled roasted peppers in oil, drained
- 2 tsp rose (or ordinary) harissa paste
- handful of mint leaves
- handful of shelled pistachio nuts
- grated zest of 1 orange plus a squeeze of juice
- 1 tsp ground cinnamon
- sea salt and freshly ground black pepper

Indian
Tomato and Tamarind Paste

Flash Substitute: bought medium curry paste (Patak's) and/or imli (tamarind sauce).

- 80g sun-dried tomatoes
- 2 tsp medium curry paste
- 1 tsp tamarind paste
- handful of coriander leaves
- squeeze of lime juice
- 1/2 tbsp olive oil, to bind
- freshly ground black pepper

Far Eastern
Sweet Satay Paste

Mix the peanut butter, honey and chives to a smooth paste with coconut milk or coconut cream. Season with soy sauce and fish sauce, and chilli powder if using.
Flash Substitute: sweet miso paste

- 3 tbsp smooth (no-added-sugar) peanut butter
- 1-2 tsp runny honey
- 1 tbsp chopped chives
- coconut milk or cream
- dash of soy sauce
- dash of nam pla fish sauce
- chilli powder to taste (optional)

Umami
Prosciutto and Parmesan Paste

Flash Substitute:
Taste #5 Umami Paste

- 65g lean prosciutto di Parma
- 45g Parmigiano Reggiano
- 2 long strips of lemon zest
- 3 tbsp extra virgin olive oil
- 5g flat-leaf parsley leaves
- splash of warm water, to blend

Finishing Salts

Add the following ingredients to 40g sea salt flakes and blend together using either a pestle and mortar or a small coffee grinder. Sprinkle them just before serving to add piquancy and for decoration.

Western
Vanilla and Black Pepper Salt

_ **1 vanilla pod**
_ **1 tsp black peppercorns**

Middle Eastern
Pink Peppercorn and Sumac Salt

_ **1 tsp sumac**
_ **1 tsp pink peppercorns**

Indian
Coriander and Fennel Salt

_ **1 tsp coriander seeds**
_ **1 tsp fennel seeds**
_ **1/2 tsp turmeric (optional, for a healthful colour)**

Far Eastern
Tea and Sichuan Peppercorn Salt

_ **1 tsp lapsang souchong or matcha tea**
_ **1 tsp Sichuan peppercorns**

Umami
Mushroom and Garlic Salt

_ **1 tbsp dried wild mushrooms**
_ **1 tsp garlic powder**

Finishing Yogurts

Stir these into soups or set a dollop in the centre of each bowl, or sit them on the side of a plate to give a refreshing finish to fish, meat and vegetable dishes. Add the ingredients shown to 3 tablespoons of live Greek-style yogurt for enough to serve 2-3 people.

Western
Pesto and Parsley Yogurt

- 1 tsp sun-dried tomato paste or pesto (green or red)
- 1 tbsp chopped flat-leaf parsley
- drizzle of balsamic vinegar

Middle Eastern
Harissa and Mint Yogurt

- 1 tsp harissa paste or powder (rose or ordinary)
- grated zest of 1 lemon and a squeeze of juice
- 1 tbsp chopped mint leaves
- 1 tsp crushed rose petals (optional)

Indian
Turmeric and Chutney Yogurt

- 1 tsp ground turmeric
- 1 tbsp chopped coriander leaves
- 1 tsp mango and/or lime chutney

Far Eastern
Matcha and Lime Yogurt

Try adding a pinch of wasabi for an unexpected ninja kick!

- 1 tsp matcha tea
- 1 tbsp chopped chives
- grated zest of 1 whole lime and a squeeze of juice
- some dried shiso (optional)

Umami
Umami Paste and Walnut Yogurt

- 1 good squeeze of Taste #5 Umami Paste
- handful of chopped toasted walnuts
- 1 tbsp chopped flat-leaf parsley
- freshly ground black pepper to taste

Props and Dressings

Props

Flash props are the ultimate food 'accessory'. Simply sprinkle these over your food for that last-minute, head-turning *je ne sais quoi*.

Western Dried Lavender Gremolata	_ zest of 1 lemon, finely chopped _ zest of 1 orange, finely chopped _ handful of flat-leaf parsley, finely chopped _ 1 garlic clove, finely chopped _ 1/2 tsp dried lavender
Middle Eastern	_ dried rose petals or chopped shelled pistachio nuts
Indian	_ dried marigold petals and edible gold
Far Eastern	_ furikake

Dressings

Aside from the odd splash of sesame oil, I use olive oil for most things (not extra virgin, which I use only when it is not going to be exposed to high temperatures) because it suits me. See Flash Fats on page 162.

Add the following ingredients to 3 tablespoons of extra virgin olive oil. For those of you who (like me) love garlic, add a single peeled and squashed (but still whole) clove to infuse flavour rather than halitosis. Finish all but the Far Eastern Ginger Vinaigrette by seasoning to taste with sea salt and freshly ground black pepper.

Each makes enough to dress a salad or other dish for 2.

Western Mustard Vinaigrette	_ 1 tbsp red/white wine vinegar _ 1/2 tsp Dijon mustard _ handful of chopped fresh herbs (optional)
Middle Eastern Pomegranate Vinaigrette	_ 1 tsp pomegranate molasses _ large pinch of ground cumin _ juice of 1/2 lemon _ handful of mixed chopped fresh flat-leaf parsley and mint
Indian Mango Vinaigrette	_ 3 tbsp Worcestershire sauce _ 1 tsp mango chutney _ juice of 1/2 lemon _ handful of chopped fresh coriander
Far Eastern Ginger Vinaigrette	_ 1 tbsp sesame oil or olive oil _ 1 tbsp soy sauce _ 1 tsp runny honey _ 2.5cm/1 inch piece of fresh ginger root, grated _ juice of 1 lime
Umami Umami Vinaigrette	_ 2 tsp Taste #5 Umami Paste _ juice of 1/2 lemon _ handful of chopped flat-leaf parsley

Lick the World

Flash	Western	Middle Eastern	Indian	Far Eastern	Umami
Seasoning	Herbes de Provence	Baharat	Garam Masala	Five-spice Powder	Taste #5 Umami Dust
Glaze	Balsamic	Pomegranate	Tamarind	Soy	Taste #5 Umami Paste
Rubinade	Rosemary & Sage	Mint, Lemon & Harissa	Curry & Coriander	Ginger & Chilli	Paprika & Taste # 5 Umami Paste
Paste	Artichoke & Caper	Red Pepper & Orange	Tomato & Tamarind	Sweet Satay	Prosciutto & Parmesan or Taste #5 Umami Paste
Finishing Salt	Vanilla & Black Pepper	Pink Peppercorn & Sumac	Coriander & Fennel	Tea & Sichuan Peppercorn	Mushroom & Garlic
Finishing Yogurt	Pesto & Parsley	Harissa & Mint	Turmeric & Chutney	Matcha & Lime	Umami Paste & Walnut
Prop	Dried Lavender Gremolata	Dried rose petals	Dried marigold petals & edible gold	Furikake	Toasted chopped walnuts
Dressing	Mustard	Pomegranate	Mango	Ginger	Umami

This simple grid is designed to illustrate how easy it is to Flash fit fast flavours in your pan. Study it and you will have the whole world licked. Play saucepan sudoku by mixing and matching flavours until you find your winning formulas. Learn to recognise the key flavours of the four corners of the world in the four corners of your local shop or supermarket.

Transformation is everything

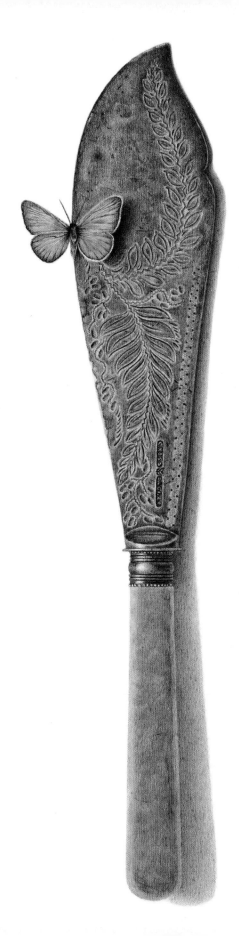

RA A ST

PAULINE NGUYEN

Il Cucchiaio d'argento

nobu THE COOKB

N WHO LOVE TOO MUCH   0·671·62049·5·450
ROBIN NORWOOD

cina
amore   Rizzoli

FOOD RULES   AN EATER'S MANUAL

Sufi Cuisine

cina e l'Arte di mangiar bene   Artusi

Flash

Recipes

This chapter is packed with my favourite world recipes, each of which illustrates the power of simple flavours. Everyday international ingredients are interestingly combined for quick, delicious and visually appetising results. The use of the word 'Flash' in front of a recipe title means that you can explore the four world cuisines by simply swapping Flash flavours (see pages 156-7).

All the recipes serve two people, except for those in the Soups and Entertaining sections, which are for four.

I am obliged to put in quantities, but I hope that once you get into Flash cooking, you will go on to remake these recipes using your own palate and visual instinct rather than tricky weights and measures.

Following the Flash Plate Rule (page 8), serve each dish with plenty of steamed or boiled leafy green veg or salad, with a drizzle of olive oil and lemon juice, or a tablespoon of a Flash Dressing (page 23) or a little butter.

Flash is not a 21-day diet plan but a way of life, so although we know that grilling, steaming and baking are best for us, I have introduced some simple pan-seared food for a more realistic plan for life. That said, if you are looking to transform yourself, see page 159.

Flash

Fish

Keep the motion in the ocean by always trying to ensure you buy sustainable fish – ask your fishmonger plus check labels in supermarkets.

Flash and Sexy Simple Grills

any fish fillets or steaks, etc
oil for cooking (optional)
Flash Seasoning (page 12)
Flash Finishing Salt (page 19)
freshly ground black pepper
good-quality extra virgin olive oil, for drizzling
lemon or lime wedges
Flash Props, Finishing Yogurts Pastes or Dressings (pages 17-23, optional)

This is the quickest recipe in the book, which is why it is worthwhile either making your own Flash Seasonings as described on page 12 and storing them for endless opportunities to impress, or stocking up on their commercial versions. Chicken fillets done this way are illustrated on page 18.

You can also make such simple grills with all sorts of meats, such as turkey escalopes, chicken breasts or mini fillets, beef steaks, veal escalopes or pork loin steaks.

1 Lightly season any of the fish fillets, steaks, etc with one of the Flash Seasonings and grill or pan-fry in a lightly oiled pan until cooked to taste.
2 Place on a serving dish and season with the Finishing Salt and pepper and drizzle with a little extra virgin olive oil. Serve with lemon wedges.
3 If you really want to push the boat out, garnish with one or two of the Flash Props, Finishing Yogurts, Pastes or Dressings.

Classic Ceviche

350g skinless, boneless very fresh fish, cut into 5cm/1 cubes
juice of 3 lemons
juice of 3 limes
juice of 1 orange
1 garlic clove, crushed
1 fresh red chilli pepper, deseeded and finely chopped
handful of coriander, chopped
handful of flat-leaf parsley, finely chopped
sea salt and freshly ground black pepper
1 red onion, thinly sliced
1 Baby Gem lettuce, to serve

For this treatment the fish must be very fresh and not have been frozen. You can also do as the Peruvians do and serve the marinade, which they call *leche de tigre* (tiger's milk), in a small glass with the ceviche. You can also ceviche large scallops.

1 Combine all the ingredients except the onion and lettuce and mix well.
2 Place the onion slices on the top, cover and refrigerate for at least 2-3 hours.
3 Serve chilled in the Baby Gem leaves.

Note: For a quick Flash transformation prepare as above but without the orange juice, then add some chopped tomatoes, peppers and mint, with a generous splash of vodka and the juice of an extra lime.

Quick Taste #5 Umami Paste Tuna Teriyaki

- 2 tuna steaks
- 2 tsp Taste #5 Umami Paste
- 3 tbsp olive oil
- freshly ground black pepper
- 3 garlic cloves, thinly sliced
- about 5 tbsp mirin (Japanese rice wine)
- about 2 tbsp soy sauce
- knob of butter

to serve
- furikake or sesame seeds
- lime wedges

The ratio of mirin to soy sauce should be around 2:1, even when splashing. This recipe is also delicious using beef or venison steaks, as well as Portobello mushroom steaks. The umami paste can be replaced with sun-dried tomato paste.

1 Rub 1 or 2 teaspoons of Taste #5 Umami Paste into each steak (depending on size but enough for it really to flavour the fish). Drizzle with olive oil on both sides, and add a good grinding of pepper. If time permits, leave to marinate for 20 minutes and for the steaks to come to room temperature.
2 Heat a non-stick frying pan with a little oil in it and, when hot, add the garlic slices. Cook the steaks on both sides to your taste (I like to sear the outside and leave the inside slightly blue).
3 Just before your steaks are cooked to taste, splash with a good glug of mirin and a splash of soy sauce (observing the 2:1 rule as per the note above). Remove the steaks from the pan and leave to rest on a warmed plate.
4 Lower the heat under the pan and deglaze it with another splash each of mirin and soy sauce, and another smaller squeeze of Taste #5 Umami Paste. Add a knob of butter, stir and pour this delicious glossy sauce over each steak.
5 Serve topped with furikake or sesame seeds and with some lime wedges on the side.

Tortured Sole

- **1 dover sole (about 550g), filleted, or 4 large lemon sole fillets**
- **1 courgette**
- **4 basil leaves**
- **3 tbsp olive oil**
- **sea salt and freshly ground black pepper**
- **lemon wedges, to serve**

for the garnishes
- **4 cherry tomatoes**

or
- **4 raw king prawn tails**

or
- **4 black olives, each with a squeeze of Taste #5 Umami Paste or sun-dried tomato paste**

or
- **4 raw scallops, preferably with their coral**

I have given you this recipe in its most basic format, but it can be jazzed up by spreading the courgette slice with any of the pastes on page 17 and/or any of the glazes on page 13. This simple version is lovely with a drizzle of any of the dressings on page 23.

1. Preheat the oven to 180°C (fan 160°C)/350°F/gas mark 4.
2. Lay each fillet out on a chopping board.
3. Cut 4 slices of courgette lengthways as thick as a pound coin.
4. Top each fillet with a courgette slice and a basil leaf, then roll up. Secure each roll with toothpicks as shown.
5. Stuff the centre of each roll with your garnish of choice and place them in an ovenproof dish. Drizzle each with a little olive oil and season with salt and pepper.
6. Bake until the fish turns opaque, 7-10 minutes.
7. Serve with lemon wedges.

Furikake-crusted Tuna
with Ginger Dressing and
Matcha Horseradish

- 2 lean tuna steaks
- 1 tbsp sesame oil
- 4 tbsp furikake mix (if you can't get this, replace it with plain toasted sesame seeds)
- 1 spring onion, finely shredded into wispy matchsticks
- 1/3 cucumber, deseeded and cut into fine matchsticks
- Ginger Dressing (page 23)

for the matcha horseradish
- 3 tbsp crème fraîche or live Greek-style yogurt
- 1/2 tsp matcha green tea
- 1 tsp bottled horseradish or a pinch of wasabi
- salt

This treatment also works brilliantly with beef fillet.

1 Brush the tuna steaks all over with the sesame oil and press them into the furikake mix to coat them all over in it.
2 Sear the tuna in a hot lightly oiled pan for about 20 seconds on each side until the sesame seeds brown but do not burn and the outer crust is firm. The idea is that the outside is cooked but the inside is still blue.
3 Serve topped with spring onion and cucumber, and drizzled with Ginger Dressing, with the matcha horseradish on the side.

Quick Fish Tartare

- 350g very fresh organic salmon or tuna fillet, finely chopped
- 1 tbsp chopped capers
- 1 tbsp finely chopped red onion (optional)
- 1 tbsp chopped chives
- 1 tbsp chopped dill
- grated zest and juice of 1 lemon
- 3 tbsp extra virgin olive oil
- squeeze of Taste #5 Umami Paste or splash of Worcestershire sauce

This dish combines the freshness of sashimi with the intense flavour of traditional steak tartare.

1 Combine all the ingredients and serve immediately.

Flash Baharat Prawn Sizzlers with Harissa Finishing Yogurt

- 200g raw king prawn tails
- 2 tbsp olive oil
- 1 tbsp baharat (page 12)
- sea salt and freshly ground black pepper
- 3 garlic cloves, thinly sliced
- 1/2 red onion, thinly sliced
- squeeze of lemon juice or splash of white wine
- handful of chopped flat-leaf parsley
- 1 bag of prewashed mixed leaf salad
- Middle Eastern Dressing (page 23)
- Harissa and Mint Finishing Yogurt (page 21)
- lemon wedges, to serve
- handful of pomegranate seeds (optional)
- chopped fresh mint (optional)

To ring the changes in this versatile recipe, simply replace the baharat with any of the other Flash seasonings and their regionally complementing dressings and yogurts.

1 Drizzle the prawns with a little of the oil and season with baharat and a little salt and pepper, ensuring they are all evenly coated.
2 Heat the remaining oil in a wok and, when hot, add the garlic and onion. Cook until softened and the garlic begins to colour, then increase the heat and add the prawns with the lemon juice or wine.
3 When the prawns are cooked through (be careful not to overcook them or they will get tough), add the parsley and adjust the seasoning.
4 Toss and serve.
5 Serve with a side salad of mixed leaves with the Middle Eastern Dressing, Harissa Finishing Yogurt and a lemon wedge. If you like, scatter with pomegranate seeds and mint for extra flavour and decoration.

Flash Ma-Yo-crusted Salmon

a little olive oil
2 firm fillets of salmon
(or cod or haddock)
sea salt and freshly ground
black pepper
$^1\!/_2$ tbsp light mayonnaise
1 $^1\!/_2$ tbsp live Greek-style
yogurt
grated zest of 1 lime and a
squeeze of juice, plus more
lime wedges to serve
$^1\!/_2$ tbsp furikake or sesame
seeds, plus more for sprinkling
$^1\!/_2$ tbsp chopped chives

This creamy and light combination of yogurt and mayonnaise provides a delicious wheat-free crust for any fish or chicken fillets. This quick topping can be flavoured with any Flash Seasoning or bought condiment such as pesto, harissa or garam masala, and enhanced with additions such as chopped fresh herbs and nuts.

1   Preheat the oven to 180°C (fan 160°C)/350°F/gas mark 4.
2   Brush an ovenproof dish with a little olive oil to stop the fish from sticking and place the fillets in it. Season each with a little salt and pepper.
3   Mix the mayonnaise, yogurt, lime zest and juice, seeds and chives together in a bowl.
4   Top the fillets with this mixture to make a crust about a 5mm ($^1\!/_4$ inch) thick.
5   Cover with foil and place in the oven for 10 minutes, then remove the foil and leave in the oven for a further 5 minutes, or until golden and bubbling, and the fish is cooked through.
6   Serve with lime wedges on the side.

International Jerk Prawn

- glug of olive oil
- ½-1 tsp jerk seasoning (depending on how hot you like it!)
- 400g peeled raw king prawn tails
- 200g mixed chopped mango and pineapple (you can use supermarket ready-cut, but cut into bite-sized pieces)
- 1 ripe banana, peeled and sliced
- salt
- knob of butter
- handful of chopped coriander leaves
- 1 red chilli, sliced and deseeded
- juice of ½ lime

I like to chop my own fruit when I am not in a hurry and I buy the small pineapples and serve my International Jerk on his own pineapple yacht.

1 Heat the oil in a non-stick wok. Add the jerk seasoning and fry for a couple of seconds. Add the prawns and toss them until coated in the jerk seasoning and almost cooked.
2 Add the fruit and season with salt to taste. When the fruit begins to soften, add the butter and stir-fry until the banana almost disappears into the sauce and the remaining fruit is hot right through.
3 Just before serving, check and adjust the seasoning, then add the coriander, chilli and a squeeze of lime juice.

Cumin-spiced Halibut Steaks with Mango Salsa

1 tsp cumin seeds
1/4 tsp Maldon salt flakes
2 halibut steaks
freshly ground black pepper
olive oil
lime wedges, to serve
Turmeric Finishing Yogurt
(page 21)

for the Mango Salsa
1 mango, peeled and
stone removed
1/2 red onion
handful of coriander leaves,
chopped
2 tbsp extra virgin olive oil
grated zest and juice
of 1 lime
sea salt and freshly ground
black pepper

For an even quicker version of this, sear the steaks in a lightly oiled pan. Serve with lemon wedges, a scattering of chopped coriander and the Turmeric Finishing Yogurt.

1 Preheat the oven to 180°C (fan 160°C)/350°F/gas mark 4.
2 To make the salsa: chop the mango flesh and onion into small, finger-nail-sized cubes. Mix together in a bowl. Add the coriander, oil and lime zest and juice. Season to taste and leave to stand in the fridge while preparing the fish and finishing yogurt. This allows the juices to be released and the flavours to mingle.
3 Mix the cumin seeds and salt together. Season each fillet on both sides with the cumin mixture, place on a baking tray and drizzle with a little olive oil.
4 Cook in the oven until the fish turns opaque and is cooked though, about 10-15 minutes.
5 Serve with a drizzle of extra-virgin olive oil, accompanied by the Mango Salsa, wedges of lime and the Turmeric Finishing Yogurt on the side.

Smoked Paprika and Orange Tuna Steaks

- 1/2 tsp smoked or ordinary paprika
- 1/2 tsp sea salt flakes
- 1/2 tsp crushed black peppercorns
- 2 tbsp olive oil
- grated zest of 1 orange and a squeeze of juice, plus 2 thin slices for garnish
- 2 tuna steaks
- splash of sweet sherry
- knob of butter
- sprinkling of finely chopped flat-leaf parsley
- 2 dollops of low-fat crème fraîche

Try serving this with a simple salad of watercress, sliced orange, sliced fennel and sliced red onion, dressed with a little olive oil and red wine vinegar.

1. Using a pestle and mortar, grind together the paprika, salt and cracked peppercorns. Stir in the olive oil and orange zest.
2. Rub the paprika mixture into the tuna steaks on both sides and, if time permits, leave to marinate for half an hour.
3. Heat a non-stick pan until hot and sear the steaks on both sides until cooked to taste. Remove the steaks and leave to sit on warmed plates while you quickly make the sauce.
4. Reduce the heat under the pan and deglaze it with a splash of sherry, a squeeze of orange juice and the knob of butter. Heat and stir until the sauce is thickened and glossy.
5. Dress each steak with a thin slice of orange and pour the sauce over them. Serve with a dollop of crème fraîche, a sprinkling of finely chopped parsley and a further dusting of paprika.

Sumac-spiced Fish with Strawberry Salsa

- 1 tbsp sumac
- 1/4 tsp sea salt flakes
- 1/2 tsp pink peppercorns
- 2 firm white fish fillets or steaks
- olive oil
- Harissa Finishing Yogurt (page 21), to serve

for the Strawberry Salsa
- 1 punnet of strawberries
- 1/2 cucumber
- 1/2 red onion
- handful of chopped coriander
- handful of chopped mint
- 3 tbsp extra virgin olive oil
- juice of 1 lime
- sea salt and freshly ground black pepper

For an ultra-quick result, simply season the fish with a sprinkling each of sumac, salt and pepper, then sear in a lightly oiled pan. Serve with lemon wedges, a scattering of chopped mint and the Harissa Finishing Yogurt.

1. Preheat the oven to 180°C (fan 160°C)/350°F/gas mark 4.
2. To make the salsa: chop the strawberries, cucumber and red onion into small, finger-nail-sized cubes and mix together in a bowl. Add the herbs, oil and lime juice. Season to taste and leave to stand in the fridge while preparing the fish and finishing yogurt. This allows the juices to be released and the flavours to mingle.
3. Using a pestle and mortar, grind the sumac together with the salt and pink peppercorns. Season each fillet on both sides with the mixture and place on a baking tray. Drizzle with a little olive oil.
4. Cook in the oven for 10-15 minutes until the fish turns opaque and is cooked though.
5. Serve drizzled with a little olive oil, with the salsa and finishing yogurt on the side.

Lemon Pesto Scallops

- olive oil
- 1-2 garlic cloves, thinly sliced
- 6-8 king scallops or 200g smaller scallops
- sea salt and freshly ground black pepper
- splash of white wine
- grated zest of 1 lemon and a squeeze of juice, plus lemon wedges to serve
- 145g fresh green pesto (the type found in the chilled section, not jars) or see below

1 Heat a dash of oil in a wok until quite hot, then add the garlic and scallops with a good grinding of black pepper.
2 When sizzling, splash with the white wine and scatter over the lemon zest. Then toss until the garlic begins to colour and scallops are opaque.
3 When the scallops are just firm but not overcooked, remove from the heat and stir in the pesto with a squeeze of lemon juice.
4 Serve immediately.

Classic Pesto Recipe For Those Who Can Be Bothered

- 2 large handfuls of basil leaves
- 1-2 garlic cloves
- 1-2 tbsp toasted pine nuts
- sea salt and freshly ground black pepper
- 30g grated pecorino cheese
- 30g grated Parmesan cheese
- extra virgin olive oil

A more delicate and perhaps more 'naïve' pesto can be achieved by leaving out the cheese and pine nuts. For red pesto, replace the basil with 2 handfuls of sun-dried tomatoes (and a sprinkling of chilli flakes if you like).

1 Place the basil leaves in a mortar with the garlic, pine nuts and a pinch of salt. Crush the ingredients to release their flavours, taking care not to be rough, as this will spoil the texture.
2 Add the cheeses and pour in a fine steady stream of olive oil, stirring until you reach your chosen consistency. Check the seasoning and adjust if necessary.

Flash The Maharaja's Secret

- 2 firm fillets of white fish, such as cod or haddock
- sea salt and freshly ground black pepper
- 2 tsp tamarind paste
- 2 slices of lime (about the thickness you would put in a drink), plus some lime wedges to serve
- 1/4 red onion, thinly sliced
- 2 slices of fresh ginger root, each about 5cm (2 inches) long, cut into matchstick strips
- 2 garlic cloves, thinly sliced
- 1 large green chilli, deseeded and thinly sliced (if you want extra heat don't deseed)
- 6 dried curry leaves
- 1 tsp ground coriander seeds
- 2 tbsp olive oil
- 2 small knobs of butter (each about 15g/1/2oz)

There are many secrets in the world of flavour, discover more – go to pages 156-7 and see how this recipe can be flashed around the world. These aromatic fish parcels should be served still wrapped up on the plate, so that the wonderful aromas that waft from inside can be enjoyed at the table as they are opened.

1 Preheat the oven to 180°C (fan160°C)/350°F/gas mark 4.
2 Place the fillets in the centre of a 30cm (12 inch) square of baking parchment (not greaseproof paper as this will tear) and season with salt and pepper.
3 Smear with the tamarind paste, place the lime slices in the centre and scatter over the onion, ginger, garlic, chilli, curry leaves and coriander. Drizzle with the oil and add the butter.
4 Close the parcel by bringing two opposite edges up together and folding over, like wrapping a parcel, then twist each end and fold in to ensure that none of the lovely juices will escape.
5 Place in the oven and cook for around 15-20 minutes, until the fish is cooked through and firm to the touch.
6 Serve with lime wedges on the side.

Tea-steamed Sea Bass with Vanilla Star Anise Olive Oil

- 2 tbsp lapsang souchong or jasmine tea
- 2 sea bass fillets, each about 170g, any pin bones removed and the skin scored
- salt

for the Vanilla Star Anise Oil
- 200ml extra virgin olive oil
- 2 vanilla pods
- 4 star anise
- 1 garlic clove, peeled
- 1 tsp black peppercorns

for the Ginger Vinegar
- 3 slices of fresh ginger, each about 2.5cm (1 inch) long, cut into thin matchstick strips
- 2 tbsp Chinese rice vinegar

Cristian Gardin, the executive chef at Santini London, taught me this delicate and remarkable 'fusion' way with olive oil. Here I have used it with simple tea-smoked sea bass, but the treatment also works beautifully with poached or steamed chicken fillets.

1 First make the Vanilla Star Anise Oil: place the oil in a small pan. Cut the vanilla pods in half lengthways and remove the seeds by running the edge of a knife along each open pod. Add these to the oil, together with the star anise, garlic and peppercorns. Heat gently over a very low heat for an hour slowly to unlock the flavours of the aromatics but not cook them. The oil should never come anywhere near the boil. Remove from the heat and set aside.
2 While that heats, make the ginger vinegar: place the ginger matchsticks in a small dish and cover with the vinegar.
3 Fill the base of a steamer with 500ml water and heat. When the water is boiling, add the tea to the water. Place the bass fillets skin-side up in the steamer and steam until cooked through but still firm, about 3-5 minutes.
4 Remove the fish from the steamer and place on a warmed serving dish. Season with a little salt, then drizzle with the Vanilla Star Anise Oil.
5 Add 2 teaspoons of the tea-infused fish water to the ginger vinegar and serve in a little dish at the table. The idea is that each person adds a teaspoon of this just before eating, Chinese dumpling-style.

Maple-glazed Salmon

- 60ml maple syrup
- 1 tbsp soy sauce
- 1 garlic clove, crushed
- pinch of ground ginger
- sea salt and freshly ground black pepper
- 2 salmon fillets

This is my favourite way with salmon and we usually have it at least once a week. Take care not to overdo the maple syrup (very tempting, I know) as the dish loses something if it is too sweet. This treatment also works very well with chicken thighs and even roasting vegetables.

1 In a small bowl, mix together the maple syrup, soy sauce, garlic and ginger, and season to taste with salt and pepper.
2 Place the salmon fillets in an ovenproof dish and coat them on all sides with the mixture. If time permits, cover with cling film and leave to marinate in the fridge for half an hour to an hour.
3 When ready to cook, preheat the oven to 200°C (fan 180°C)/400°F/gas mark 6. Cook the salmon in the ovenproof dish, uncovered, for around 15-20 minutes, until its centre is cooked through.

Oven-roasted Monkfish
With Cherry Tomato Topping

- 350-400g monkfish tail, trimmed
- 2 handfuls of green beans
- sea salt and freshly ground black pepper
- squeeze of lemon juice
- handful of lemon thyme or plain thyme
- drizzle of olive oil

for the topping
- 4 tbsp extra virgin olive oil
- good squeeze of lemon juice to taste
- dash of Worcestershire sauce
- splash of balsamic vinegar
- handful of chopped chives
- handful of chopped basil
- handful of chopped flat-leaf parsley
- 30g wild rocket, torn
- 2 garlic cloves, halved
- 250g cherry tomatoes, quartered

This dish is best served warm and not piping-hot, so there is time to make that all-important call just before dinner! If you can't get all the herbs, just increase the rocket.

1   Preheat the oven to 180°C (fan 160°C)/350°F/gas mark 4.
2   Cut the monkfish into 4 medallions, each about 1.5cm (3/4inch) thick (ask the fishmonger to do this for you).
3   Place the beans in an ovenproof dish, sit the monkfish on top of the beans and season with salt and pepper. Add a squeeze of lemon juice and a few sprigs of thyme. Drizzle with oil and bake for 15 minutes or until the fish is cooked through but the beans still have a bite.
4   While the fish and beans are cooking, prepare the topping: mix the oil, lemon juice, Worcestershire sauce and balsamic vinegar. Finely chop together all the herbs except the rocket. Add these to the dressing, together with the garlic and chopped tomatoes. Season with salt and pepper.
5   Place 2 monkfish medallions on a bunch of beans on each plate. Add the rocket to the dressed tomato topping and spoon over the monkfish.

Provence-seasoned Cod Fillet with
Garlic Butter and Lavender Gremolata

- 2 large cod fillets, preferably skin on
- 1 tsp Herbes de Provence (page 12)
- sea salt and freshly ground black pepper
- olive oil

to serve
- 2 knobs of bought garlic butter
- Dried Lavender Gremolata (page 23)

See also pages 22-25 for how this simple dish can be given a world of different flavour treatments.

1 Preheat the oven to 180°C (fan160°C)/350°F/gas mark 4.
2 Season the fish on both sides with the herbs, salt and pepper.
3 Place on a baking tray and drizzle with a little olive oil. Bake for about 10-15 minutes, until the fish is just firm, cooked through and no longer translucent.
4 Serve with a small knob of garlic butter and a sprinkling of Lavender Gremolata.

Classic Garlic Butter Recipe For
Those Who Can Be Bothered

- 100g salted butter, softened
- 1 tbsp chopped flat-leaf parsley
- 3 garlic cloves
- grated zest of 1 lemon (optional)
- sea salt and freshly ground black pepper

If you want, you can make your own garlic butter to keep in the fridge – it has all sorts of uses with all sorts of foods.

1 In a bowl, cream the butter with the other ingredients. Adjust the seasoning.
2 Roll the mixture into a sausage shape, wrap in cling film and chill in the fridge until firm.
3 Unwrap and slice into thickish discs to use.

If I can give up sugar I can give up you

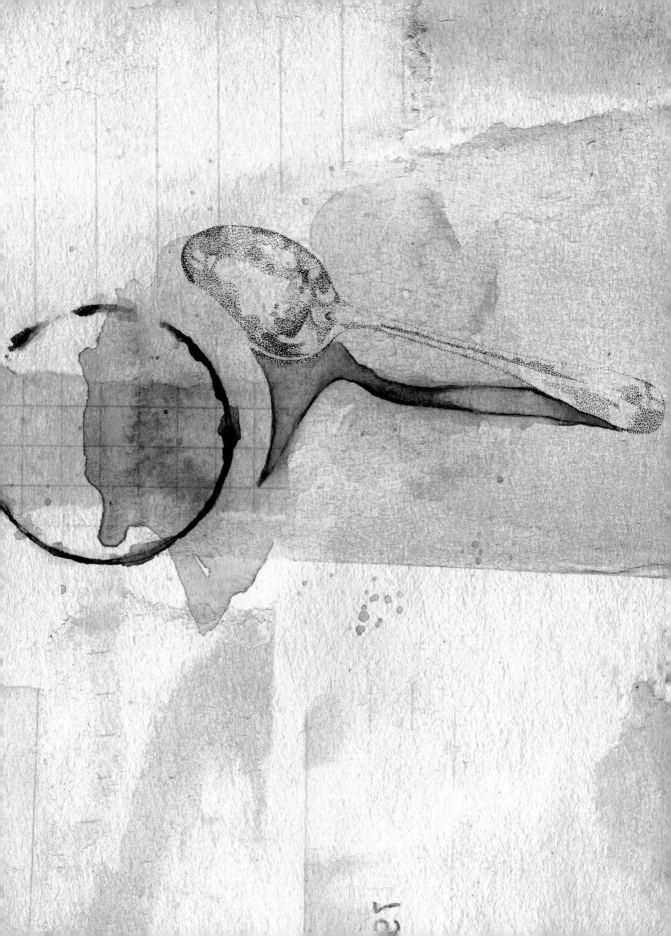

Flash

Flesh

In the Flash way, it is best to restrict the eating of red meat to 2-3 meals a week, but I've included my favourite recipes for those days. I recommend using free-range poultry and grass-reared meats when possible, plus a little game for its healthy lack of fat.

Pork Cutlets with Sage and Anchovy Butter

4 lean pork fillet medallions, cut into rounds about 1cm (1/2 inch) thick
2 tsp Herbes de Provence
sea salt and freshly ground black pepper
olive oil

for the Sage and Anchovy Butter
40g butter
2 canned salted anchovies, drained
1 garlic clove, squashed but whole
9 sage leaves

Underdone pork is a no-no, but fillet of pork cooks in a matter of minutes and can become tough if overcooked, so this dish is all about finding the perfect balance! This dish also works well with veal fillet.

For dinner parties I often get two loins (about 1kg) for four and rub the outside of each loin with olive oil and season with salt, freshly ground black pepper and Herbes de Provence. I then colour each loin in a lightly oiled frying pan until brown on all sides, sprinkle with a little more herbs and finish with 8-10 minutes in an oven preheated oven to 180°C (fan 160°C)/350°F/gas mark 4, until cooked through. The fillets can then be sliced at the table and the Sage and Anchovy Butter spooned over at that point.

1 First make the sage and anchovy butter: place the butter, anchovies, garlic and sage leaves in a small heavy-based pan and heat gently until the anchovies have dissolved into the melted butter and the sage and garlic have infused their flavours. Do not allow this to sizzle at any time.
2 Dust the pork medallions with a sprinkling of the herbs, a very little salt (the anchovy is quite salty) and some pepper. Cook in a lightly oiled pan for a couple of minutes on both sides until cooked through and golden on the outside.
3 Serve 2 medallions per person, with a little Sage and Anchovy Butter spooned over.

Quick Turkey Tonnato

200g bought thinly sliced
cooked turkey (or chicken)

for the Tonnato Sauce
- 2 tbsp low-fat mayonnaise
  (or 3 tbsp mayonnaise and
  no yogurt)
- 1 tbsp Greek-style yogurt
- 50g canned tuna in brine or
  spring water, drained
- squeeze of Taste #5 Umami
  Paste
- squeeze of lemon juice, plus
  lemon wedges to serve
- sea salt and freshly ground
  black pepper

to garnish
- sprinkling of small capers
- sprigs of fresh dill or a
  scattering of crushed
  pink peppercorns

This quick tonnato sauce is also delicious over hard-boiled eggs. The Taste #5 Umami Paste can also be replaced here with 1 salted anchovy fillet (in oil, drained) and 1 tablespoon of small capers, both drained.

1 For the tonnato sauce, place all the ingredients except the lemon juice and seasonings in a small food processor or blend with a stick blender until smooth. Dilute to the consistency to make it suitable for coating the meat by means of a squeeze of lemon juice and a splash of water, if necessary. Season to taste.
2 Arrange the meat slices on two plates and spread over the sauce.
3 Garnish with a sprinkling of capers and a couple of sprigs of dill or a scattering of crushed pink peppercorns. Serve with a lemon wedge on the side.

Tandoori-style Chicken

6 boneless skinless chicken
thigh fillets
lime wedges, to serve

for the Tandoori Marinade
150g low-fat Greek-style yogurt
1 tbsp tandoori paste or
medium curry paste
grated zest of 1 lime
and a squeeze of juice
1 tsp garam masala or
chaat masala (optional)
sea salt and freshly ground
black pepper

for the Mango and
Watercress Salad
1 ripe mango, peeled,
stone removed and flesh cut
into slices
1 bag of watercress salad
Mango Vinaigrette (page 23)

for the Mint and Cucumber Raita
125ml low-fat live
natural yogurt
¼ cucumber, grated
handful of chopped mint
sea salt and freshly ground
black pepper

This dish can be prepared in the morning and the fillets left all day, covered in the fridge, to marinate. It can also be made with diced chicken breast or mini fillets.

1 Preheat the oven to 180°C (fan 160°C)/350°F/gas mark 4.
2 Make the marinade by mixing all the ingredients together in a bowl and season to taste.
3 Coat each chicken thigh with the marinade and set aside to marinate briefly while you make the salad and raita by mixing together all their individual ingredients.
4 To cook the chicken, simply place the fillets on a baking tray and cook for 25 minutes or until cooked through. Halfway through cooking, add another spoonful of marinade on top of each fillet.
5 Serve with lime wedges, salad and the raita.

Veal Escalope with Salsa Verde

2 even-sized veal escalopes
½ tbsp olive oil
sea salt and freshly ground black pepper

for the Salsa Verde
handful each of finely chopped flat-leaf parsley, basil and mint
3 anchovy fillets in oil, drained and finely chopped (optional)
1-2 garlic cloves, crushed
2 tbsp baby capers, rinsed and drained
juice of ½ lemon or 2 tbsp white wine vinegar
½ tsp Dijon mustard
about 5 tbsp extra virgin olive oil
sea salt and freshly ground black pepper

This dish works with a variety of meats: pork or turkey escalopes are perfect, as is minute steak. Dill or chives can also be used in the Salsa Verde in place of the basil and mint. For an umami deliciousness, replace the Dijon mustard with a squeeze of Taste #5 Umami Paste.

1   First make the Salsa Verde: combine all the ingredients except the oil and seasoning in a bowl and add just enough olive oil to give a soft salsa consistency. Season with salt and pepper and set aside.
2   Make the escalopes a little thinner by placing each between two large sheets of cling film and gently bashing them with a rolling pin until slightly flattened.
3   Splash each escalope with a drizzle of olive oil on both sides and sprinkle with a little salt and pepper.
4   Heat a large non-stick griddle pan and cook the veal until coloured on both sides. Take care not to overcook it, as this will toughen the meat.
5   Top each escalope with a little Salsa Verde and serve.

Venison Tagliata with Juniper and Rosemary

- **2 venison steaks**
- **leaves from 2 sprigs of rosemary**
- **1 large garlic clove**
- **1/2 tsp juniper berries**
- **1/2 tsp salt flakes**
- **1 tsp crushed black peppercorns**
- **3 tbsp olive oil**

I love these woodland flavours with a mixed leaf and raspberry salad. Simply toss a punnet of fresh raspberries in with the leaves and dress with extra virgin olive oil and a splash of raspberry vinegar or red wine vinegar.

1 Using a pestle and mortar, grind together the garlic, rosemary, juniper berries, salt and black pepper. Then add just enough olive oil to form a loose paste.
2 Season each venison steak with a spoonful of the mixture. If time permits, cover them in cling film and leave to come to room temperature for about 20-30 minutes.
3 Preheat the grill to high and place the steaks under it. Cook both sides until the steaks are done to your taste. Remember, though, that venison, being very lean, dries out quickly if overcooked.
4 When cooked, leave the meat to rest in a warm place for a couple of minutes. Drizzle with any remaining marinade that hasn't been in contact with the raw meat, and serve.

Five-spice Minced Pork
and Tenderstem Broccoli

_ **1 tbsp sesame oil**
_ **3 garlic cloves, thinly sliced**
_ **1 tsp grated fresh ginger**
_ **1 tsp Chinese five-spice powder**
_ **500g pork mince**
_ **250g Tenderstem broccoli**
_ **4 spring onions, chopped**
_ **1 red chilli, sliced and deseeded**
_ **2 tbsp nam pla fish sauce**
_ **1/2 tbsp runny honey**
_ **juice of 1 lime**

for the garnish
_ **handful of chopped
coriander leaves**
_ **2 tbsp roughly chopped natural
roasted peanuts**
_ **2 lime wedges**

This recipe makes a little more than you need for two, but as mince usually comes in 500g packs, I have used this as a marker. Any leftovers can be tossed in a wok the next day.

1 Heat the sesame oil in wok and add the garlic, ginger and five-spice powder. When sizzling, add the pork and stir-fry until it begins to brown. Add the broccoli and continue to stir-fry until that begins to become tender.
2 Add the spring onions, chilli, fish sauce, honey and lime juice, and stir-fry until bubbling and the pork is nicely browned. Reduce the heat and allow to simmer for a minute or so until the broccoli is just tender.
3 Serve topped with fresh coriander, a sprinkling of peanuts and a wedge of lime on the side.

Duck Breasts with Black Magic Elixir

2 duck breasts
olive oil
sea salt and freshly ground
black pepper
2 small sprigs of rosemary
1 garlic clove, peeled
and halved

for the Black Chocolate Elixir
50ml thick balsamic vinegar
(I use Belazu)
5g 100% cacao (I like to use
Venezuelan Black),
coarsely grated
25ml extra virgin olive oil

The Black Chocolate Elixir spellbinds anything from steak to roasted root vegetables.

1 Preheat the oven to 200°C (fan 180°C)/400°F/gas mark 6.
2 To make the elixir, mix all the ingredients together in a bowl and leave to stand.
3 Rub the meaty side of the duck breasts with a little olive oil and season with salt and pepper.
4 Place the breasts in a baking tray, skin side up, each sitting on a sprig of rosemary and ½ garlic clove.
5 Cook in the preheated oven for 7-12 minutes for medium-cooked meat, a little longer for well-done.
6 Take the duck from the oven and remove the skin and any fat. Cut at an angle into slices and serve with a drizzle of the elixir.

Flash Stuffed Chicken Pockets with Red Pesto and Ricotta

2 skinless chicken breasts
2 tbsp ricotta cheese
6 basil leaves, finely chopped
2 tbsp red pesto
sea salt and freshly ground black pepper
2 slices of prosciutto, pancetta or streaky bacon
2 sprigs of rosemary or thyme (optional)
olive oil

for the dressing
1 tbsp extra virgin olive oil
½ tbsp balsamic vinegar

You can also stuff chicken breasts with any of the pastes on page 17, glaze with one of the glazes on page 13 and serve with one of the dressings on page 23.

1 Preheat the oven to 180°C (fan 160°C)/350°F/gas mark 4.
2 Place the chicken breasts on a chopping board (some wet kitchen roll under the board will help stop it slipping). Place your non-cutting hand flat over the breast and, using a small sharp knife, cut a small 'pocket' in the side of each breast for your stuffing, taking care not to cut right through.
3 To make stuffing, mix the ricotta, basil and 1 tablespoon of the pesto together, adding a good grinding of black pepper.
4 Carefully stuff each breast with a spoonful of the stuffing. Season the chicken breast with a little salt and pepper, and wrap it in a slice of prosciutto, pancetta or bacon to seal the pocket. If you have them, tuck the rosemary or thyme under the wrapping, then tuck the ends underneath the breast and place on a baking tray.
5 Glaze each breast with the remaining pesto mixed with a little oil to dilute it to brushing consistency and bake in the oven for 20-30 minutes, until each chicken breast is cooked right through.
6 Make the dressing by whisking the oil and vinegar together with some seasoning to taste. Drizzle this over the chicken to serve.

Umami-truffled
Steak Handkerchiefs

- 1 tbsp olive oil
- 1 beef fillet steak, sliced very thinly widthwise
- freshly ground black pepper
- 100g baby spinach leaves
- 2 tbsp coarsely grated Parmesan cheese
- furikake or toasted sesame seeds, to garnish

for the dressing
- 1 tbsp truffle oil
- squeeze of Taste #5 Umami Paste (Japanese Formula) or a dash of soy sauce
- squeeze of lemon juice

This recipe was shown to me by my friend and mentor Nobu Matsuhisa, the ultimate flavour master. He serves a similar dish in his restaurants, with the addition of a sprinkling of his dried miso powder.

1   In a wok, heat a little olive oil. When just smoking, add the beef slices and flash-fry for 1 minute, adding a little salt and black pepper. Remove from the heat and set aside to rest.
2   Make the dressing by mixing all the ingredients in a bowl and set it aside.
3   Toss the raw spinach leaves and the steak 'handkerchiefs' in the dressing mixed with the meat juices and the Parmesan cheese.
4   Serve garnished with a little furikake or toasted sesame seeds.

Preserved Lemon and Cumin Chicken Cakes

6 boneless skinless chicken
thigh fillets

1 egg yolk

1 small preserved lemon (about
the size of a ping-pong ball)

½ tbsp harissa paste or powder
(rose or ordinary)

1 tsp ground cumin

handful of flat-leaf parsley

sea salt and freshly ground
black pepper

a little olive oil for brushing
(optional)

to serve

lettuce leaves (ideally radicchio
or Baby Gem)

Harissa and Mint Finishing
Yogurt (page 21)

This recipe can also be made with 500g firm white fish, such as monkfish. As an accompaniment, try making a dipping sauce with 2 tablespoons of Chinese rice vinegar, a drop of runny honey, a couple of drops of nam pla fish sauce, a squeeze of lime juice and some shredded fresh ginger matchsticks.

1   Preheat the oven to 180°C (fan 160°C)/350°F/gas mark 4.
2   Put all ingredients except the oil in a food processor and blend to a paste. To check for seasoning, I fry a little of the mixture to taste and see if it needs more salt, as it isn't advisable to eat raw chicken. Shape into small patties.
3   Place on a non-stick or lightly oiled baking tray and cook in the preheated oven for 15-20 minutes, until golden on the outside and cooked through.
4   Serve on crisp lettuce leaves with a dollop of Harissa and Mint Finishing Yogurt on the side.

Grilled Turkey Steaks
with Chimichurri Salsa

- 2 turkey steaks
- sea salt and freshly ground black pepper
- olive oil

for the Chimichurri Salsa
- large handful of flat-leaf parsley
- large handful of coriander leaves
- 4 garlic cloves, roughly chopped
- 4 tbsp extra virgin olive oil
- 2 tbsp red wine vinegar
- juice of ½ lemon, plus lemon wedges to serve
- ¼ medium red onion, roughly chopped
- sea salt and freshly ground black pepper

The Argentinean version of salsa verde, chimichurri can be used for basting, as a marinade or as a table sauce.

1 To make the Chimichurri Salsa: blend all the ingredients together in a small blender or with a stick blender and season to taste. If you prefer, you can do this by hand-chopping the herbs and garlic finely, then adding the other ingredients. The consistency should be between that of a pesto and a dressing, so add oil as necessary.
2 Season the turkey steaks with a little salt and pepper and drizzle them with a little olive oil. Heat a grill pan and, when hot, place the steaks in the pan and cook on both sides until golden and cooked through. It looks best to have nice even markings on the steaks, so don't turn them too soon or too often.
3 Serve the steaks with a lemon wedge and a spoonful of chimichurri.

The Dog's Bolognese

- 1 tbsp olive oil
- 1 onion, finely chopped
- 2 garlic cloves, crushed
- 500g lean minced beef
- 25g tomato paste
- 1 (125ml) glass of red wine
- 25g Taste #5 Umami Paste or a dash of soy sauce
- handful of chopped fresh marjoram (or pinch of dried)
- handful of torn basil leaves
- sea salt and freshly ground black pepper

This recipe makes a little more than you need for two but since mince usually comes in 500g packs I have used this as a marker; any leftovers can be tossed in a wok the next day. This is delicious with steamed green vegetables, and a little grated Parmesan or pecorino. For a more complete meal version, add just a splash of tomato passata and some chopped vegetables – peppers, courgettes, broccoli, etc. – and stir-fry until the veg are tender but still al dente.

1 Heat the olive oil in a wok. When it is hot, add the onion. When the onions are glassy, add the garlic. When everything is sizzling, add the mince, turn up the heat and stir-fry to seal in all the flavour.
2 When the mince is browned and sizzling, add the tomato paste, wine, umami paste or soy sauce, herbs and a good grinding of black pepper, with a sprinkling of salt if needed.
3 Stir-fry for a minute or two and then the lower heat and simmer until the wine has reduced to a glaze.
4 Adjust the seasoning if necessary and serve.

Maple Mustard Chicken

- **6 boneless skinless chicken thigh fillets**

for the Umami Maple Mustard Glaze
- **4 tbsp maple syrup**
- **1½ tbsp grainy mustard**
- **1½ tbsp Dijon mustard**
- **2 tsp Herbes de Provence**
- **squeeze of Taste #5 Umami Paste or a dash of soy sauce (optional)**

My friend Janie, who gave me this recipe, says, 'You can slap this over anything and it will taste good'. Her favourite is new potatoes in their skins, but that is not very Flash although great for entertaining. Other delicious options are salmon and roasted vegetables.

1 Preheat the oven to 180°C (fan 160°C)/350°F/gas mark 4.
2 Make the glaze by mixing all the ingredients together in a bowl.
3 Place the chicken thighs in an ovenproof dish and coat each all over in the glaze, taking care to spread extra on the top of each.
4 Cook in the oven for 30 minutes, or until the thighs are cooked right through and the glaze has formed a richly coloured crust. During the cooking, spoon the glaze from the dish over the thighs to keep them moist.
5 Serve immediately.

Tasty Chicken Livers with Asparagus

- **2 tbsp olive oil**
- **squeeze of Taste #5 Umami Paste or splash of soy sauce**
- **8 chicken livers**
- **2 garlic cloves, thinly sliced**
- **leaves from 2 sprigs of fresh thyme, chopped**
- **200g asparagus spears**
- **generous splash of white wine or vermouth**
- **knob of butter (optional)**
- **sea salt flakes and freshly ground black pepper**

With the livers, asparagus and umami paste or soy sauce, this dish is a true umami feast.

1 Mix the oil with a good squeeze of Taste #5 Umami Paste or soy sauce and rub all over the livers.
2 Heat a wok and, when smoking-hot, add the chicken livers, garlic and thyme.
3 Toss until the livers are browned and sizzling on all sides. Remove them from the wok with a slotted spoon and set aside.
4 Add the asparagus spears to the hot wok and toss with a tablespoon of water until beginning to get tender. Return the livers to the wok and splash them with the wine and add the butter, if using, and some seasoning to taste. Stir-fry until the asparagus is fully tender.

- 1 medium red onion
- 500g lean minced beef
- 1 egg yolk
- bunch of flat-leaf parsley, finely chopped
- sea salt and freshly ground black pepper
- 2 large Portobello mushrooms, stalks removed
- squeeze of Taste #5 umami paste or tomato ketchup/relish
- olive oil
- 2 slices of cheese (optional)
- 4 thick slices of beef tomato
- 2 Iceberg lettuce leaves
- slices of dill pickle

for the Marie Rose Sauce
- 1 tbsp low-fat mayonnaise
- 1 tbsp low-fat Greek-style yogurt
- 1 tbsp tomato ketchup
- 1 tsp Worcestershire sauce
- 1 tsp Cognac or sherry (optional)
- dash of Tabasco
- lemon juice to taste
- pinch of paprika
- pinch of salt

The actual burger part of this recipe technically makes 4 Flash burgers. That said, if I am in the mood for a burger I confess to making it a big one and tend to make 2-3 burgers out of this quantity of meat – 2 for us and one uncooked for the freezer! You could slip a slice of goats' cheese into the stack; no one would complain.

1 Halve the onion and cut a thick slice from each, then separate these into rings and set aside. Finely chop the remaining onion.
2 In a large bowl, mix together the chopped onion with the minced beef, egg yolk and parsley. Season well and divide the mixture into two chunky burgers. Cover with cling film and chill for 25-30 minutes.
3 When ready to cook, preheat the oven to 180°C (fan160°C)/350°F/ gas mark 4 and make the Marie Rose Sauce by mixing together all the ingredients.
4 Place the chilled burgers on a lightly oiled tray and cook in the oven for 25 minutes.
5 Place the mushrooms on a baking tray and spread with a little Taste #5 Umami Paste, if using, and a drizzle of olive oil. Cook in the preheated oven until just softened (but not too much as this will be your bun).
6 To serve, stack in the following order from the bottom up: mushroom, umami paste or ketchup, cheese if using, tomato, lettuce, onion, dill pickle slice, burger and finally the sauce.

The Thighs The Limit with Coriander and Fennel Seeds

- 6 boneless skinless chicken thigh fillets
- drizzle of olive oil
- 1 large orange, cut into slices skin on
- Dried Lavender Gremolata (page 23, optional)

for the marinade
- 2-3 garlic cloves
- 2 tsp coriander seeds
- 2 tsp fennel seeds
- 1 tsp salt flakes
- 3 tbsp olive oil
- freshly ground black pepper

With the skin off the chicken, the random orange slices act as little protective discs to stop the meat drying out. However, if the chicken does seem to be drying out at any time, baste it with a little fresh orange juice or a splash of stock. These are lovely served with Turmeric Finishing Yogurt (page 21) with a little grated orange zest mixed into it.

1 To prepare the marinade, use a pestle and mortar to pound the garlic, coriander and fennel seeds with the salt flakes. Add the olive oil and mix to a loose paste, then season with black pepper.
2 Rub this over the chicken thighs and cover with a plate. Ideally, leave to marinate in the fridge for a few hours or overnight, with a weight on top of the plate so the flavours are literally pressed into the meat.
3 When ready to cook, preheat the oven to 180°C (fan 160°C)/350°F/ gas mark 4.
4 Place the thighs in an ovenproof dish, drizzle with olive oil and cover with orange slices.
5 Bake for 20-30 minutes until cooked through.
6 Serve with the gremolata.

Food is intimate. Intimacy is treating someone how you need to be treated

Flash

Eggs, Cheese & Tofu

These ways of getting the best from alternative Flash protein foods help break up the week and also give balance to its meals. I recommend using free-range eggs whenever possible.

Flash! Innocent Steamed Tofu

- 350g block of firm tofu, cut into 2.5cm (1-inch) thick slices
- any Flash Finishing Salt (page 19)
- any Flash Dressing (page 23)
- chopped fresh herbs

I must confess that tofu is not my favourite ingredient and I have difficulty with both its taste and texture. For this book I have worked hard to inspire myself in places I didn't think possible. I can now actually say that tofu + flavour = a healthy and tasty meal; I hope you will agree.

1 Cook the tofu in a steamer for 5-7 minutes.
2 Season with a Flash Finishing Salt, a complementing Flash Dressing and a handful of fresh herbs.

Sicilian Spicy Umami Tofu

- 1 tbsp Taste #5 Umami Paste or sun-dried tomato paste
- 1 tbsp olive oil
- squeeze of lemon juice
- 350g block of firm tofu, cut into 1cm (1/2 inch) thick slices
- 1/2 tsp chilli flakes
- handful of walnuts or flaked almonds
- 1 tbsp raisins
- large handful of rocket

Any of the Flash Pastes on page 17 can be spread on the tofu slices – about 5mm (1/4 inch) thick to give them a tasty crust when baked. Also try any of the Flash Seasonings on page 12, with a sprinkling of salt flakes and a drizzle of olive oil. Yet another idea, to give it an Oriental vibe, is to try the same recipe using Taste #5 Umami Paste and replace the lemon with lime and the walnut topping with furikake or toasted sesame seeds.

1 In a bowl, whisk together the umami paste or sun-dried tomato paste with the olive oil and squeeze of lemon juice.
2 Pour this over the tofu slices and rub it in until all sides of the slices are well covered. If time permits, leave to marinate from 20 minutes to overnight.
3 Preheat the oven to 180°C (fan160°C)/350°F/gas mark 4.
4 Sprinkle the tofu slices with the chilli flakes and place on a baking tray with the nuts. Bake in the oven for 20 minutes. Remove the nuts after 3-4 minutes and leave to cool.
5 When the nuts are cooler, roughly chop them with the raisins.
6 Remove the tofu when it is cooked and serve with a sprinkling of the chopped walnuts and raisins, and a scatter of rocket leaves.

Olive Oil-Fried Eggs with Paprika Chickpeas, Harissa and Yogurt

- 2 tbsp drained tinned chickpeas
- 1 tbsp olive oil, plus an extra dash for the chickpeas
- ½ tsp sweet paprika
- 4 eggs, preferably free-range
- sea salt and freshly ground black pepper
- 8 marinated black olives, drained, stoned and chopped
- 2 tbsp Greek-style yogurt
- 2 tbsp harissa paste (rose or ordinary)
- 1 tbsp chopped flat-leaf parsley

I first came across this dish at the restaurant Ammo in Los Angeles. If angels ate eggs for brunch this is how they would be cooked. You will know what I mean when you taste the hot yolk against the chilled yogurt, spicy harissa and crunchy egg white. If you need to mop up the yolk and steamed veg just doesn't cut it, try some toasted spelt sourdough bread.

1 In a small bowl, mix the chickpeas with a dash of olive oil, a sprinkling of sweet paprika and some salt to taste.

2 Heat a large non-stick frying pan and, when hot, sauté the chickpeas until golden and slightly crisp. Remove with a slotted spoon and set on some kitchen paper to absorb any excess oil.

3 Wipe the pan out with some kitchen paper and add a tablespoon of olive oil. When this is sizzling, crack the eggs into the pan and season with a little salt and pepper. Fry them on a medium heat until the edges and bottoms are crisping and bubbling, the white is cooked through and yolk is perfectly sunny.

4 Serve 2 perfect eggs on each plate with a scattering of the paprika-coated chickpeas, a sprinkling of marinated black olive pieces and a dollop each of yogurt and harissa on the side of each plate. Garnish with a little finely chopped parsley.

Taste #5 Umami Paste
Egg White Omelette

- ½ tsp olive oil
- whites of 4 eggs or 150ml Two Chicks Free Range Liquid Egg White
- 1 tbsp chopped fresh herbs, such as parsley, dill or chives
- freshly ground black pepper
- squeeze of Taste #5 Umami Paste or any of the pastes on page 17

I like to use Two Chicks Free Range Liquid Egg White, which is available in most supermarkets in chilled cartons. This simple omelette makes for a low-fat, high-protein hassle-free breakfast/meal and a brilliant backdrop for my Taste # 5 Umami Paste or any of the pastes on page 17.

1 Heat a non-stick frying pan and add the olive oil.
2 Add the egg whites and herbs, and stir in the black pepper, making sure everything is well combined.
3 When the egg whites have almost cooked, squeeze a small amount of Taste # 5 Umami paste into the eggs and gently spread with the back of a spoon. Fold the omelette over by first gently running a spatula around the edges and then lifting one half over the other.
4 Serve immediately.

Grilled Lemon Halloumi

- 2 unwaxed lemons, very thinly sliced
- 1 garlic clove, crushed
- pinch of salt flakes
- 1 tsp pink peppercorns
- 2 tbsp olive oil
- 1 tsp runny honey
- 1 tbsp small sprigs of fresh dill
- 250g block of halloumi cheese, cut into slices about 1.5cm (3/4 inch) thick

For a really quick version of this, sprinkle the cheese with any of the Flash Seasonings (page 12) or brush with a Flash Glaze (page 13). Another idea is just to sprinkle it with sesame seeds and dried mint.

1. Preheat the grill to its hottest.
2. Slice one lemon into rounds 5mm (1/4 inch) thick.
3. Using a pestle and mortar, pound the garlic with a tiny pinch of salt and the pink peppercorns. Add the olive oil, honey and a good squeeze of juice from the other lemon.
4. Rub the lemon slices and the cheese slices with the mixture.
5. Place in an ovenproof dish and set under the grill (not too close to the heat or it will burn rather than toast) until the cheese begins to colour and the lemon slices caramelize.
6. Remove from the grill, turn the lemon and cheese pieces over and return to grill the other sides in the same way.
7. Serve sprinkled with dill, and with the remaining dressing and any juices from the pan drizzled over.

Dressed Ricotta

- 250g ricotta cheese
- handful of chopped fresh mixed herbs, such as basil, mint, chervil, marjoram and parsley
- $1/2$ tsp chilli flakes (optional)
- grated zest of 1 lemon
- sea salt and freshly ground black pepper
- 1 tbsp green or black tapenade
- drizzle or two of extra virgin olive oil
- splash of wine vinegar

Serve the dressed ricotta with crunchy crudités and a big salad or steamed vegetables. The tapenade can be replaced with a light pesto in this recipe, or omitted altogether.

1 Turn the ricotta out on a serving dish. Slightly squash and spread it with the back of a fork.
2 Sprinkle with the chopped herbs, chilli flakes if using them, the lemon zest, salt and pepper.
3 Mix the tapenade with some olive oil and a splash of vinegar, then drizzle this mixture and some more extra virgin olive oil over the ricotta.

Dressed Mozzarella with Tomato and Rocket

- 2 buffalo mozzarella cheeses, each about 250g
- squeeze of Taste #5 Umami Paste or sun-dried tomato paste
- 2 tbsp olive oil
- squeeze of lemon juice
- 250g cherry tomatoes, halved
- 2 handfuls of rocket
- handful of torn basil
- sea salt and freshly ground black pepper

You can also dress the cheeses with olive oil and a dash of balsamic vinegar, a finely chopped anchovy (in oil, drained) and a scattering of baby capers. Sun-dried or sun-blush tomatoes are also delicious with this dish.

1 Place each cheese in a serving dish.
2 To make the dressing, simply whisk a squeeze of umami paste with the olive oil and a good squeeze of lemon juice.
3 Sprinkle each cheese with equal portions of cherry tomato halves and the rocket leaves.
4 Drizzle over the umami paste dressing and sprinkle on some torn basil leaves. Season to taste with pepper.

Grilled Paneer with Chaat Masala and Pineapple

200g block of paneer cheese,
cut into 1cm (1/2 inch) slices
2-3 tsp tamarind paste
1 tsp chaat masala
1 tin of pineapple slices
in juice, drained
handful of chopped coriander

to serve
mixed leaf salad
Mango Vinaigrette (page 23)

Bollywood meets Bolan in this 1970s classic combination. This makes a great nibble to serve with drinks. Unlike the '70s, paneer is a very bland cheese and requires some seasoning.

1 Preheat the grill to high.
2 Spread each cheese slice with a little tamarind paste, season with chaat masala and place on a baking tray.
3 Cut the pineapple rings in half and top each cheese slice with a piece.
4 Season each slice with another pinch of chaat masala.
5 Grill until the cheese and pineapple begin to colour.
6 Garnish with a scattering of chopped fresh coriander. Serve with a mixed leaf salad with Mango vinaigrette.

Creamy Frying Pan Scrambled Eggs with Ikura and Matcha Green Tea

4-6 large eggs, preferably
free-range or organic
sea salt and freshly ground
black pepper
knob of salted butter
2 tsp ikura (salmon eggs)
or lumpfish roe or
caviar (optional)
sprinkling of matcha green tea
red shiso leaves or chives,
to garnish

I love this served with plain steamed Tenderstem broccoli. For an even quicker version of this dish, omit the salmon eggs and do not add salt when beating the egg, but season with Tea and Sechuan Peppercorn Salt (page 23). If you don't have that to hand, just season the eggs with a little sea salt and pepper when beating and sprinkle some matcha on top at the end before serving. (I don't advise adding the matcha to the eggs when beating, as the final colour isn't too appetising.)

1 In a bowl, lightly beat the eggs with a small pinch of salt and a grinding of black pepper.
2 Heat the butter in a non-stick frying pan. When sizzling, but not coloured, add the eggs and move them around the pan with a wooden spatula (my favourite) or spoon.
3 When the eggs begin to scramble but are still runny and glossy, remove from the heat as they will continue to cook.
4 Spoon on warmed plates and top each portion with a teaspoon of the salmon eggs, a sprinkling of matcha tea and a couple of red shiso leaves or chive stalks.

I spend so much time communicating with others that I forget to communicate with myself

Flash

Comfort

Comforting and complex, this section deals mostly with carbohydrates and healthful ways to enjoy delicious wheat-free alternatives. Keep portions of them to 2 i-phones-worth and serve with mostly plants.

Quick Butter Bean Stew with Fresh Tomatoes and Olives

2 tbsp olive oil
1 onion, thinly sliced
3 garlic cloves, thinly sliced
25g fresh ginger root, finely chopped
pinch of saffron threads
16 cherry tomatoes
2 (400g) cans of cooked butter beans, drained and rinsed
$1/2$ tsp runny honey
handful of fleshy black olives (Kalamata are ideal), stoned
1 tsp ground cinnamon
1 tsp paprika
sea salt and freshly ground black pepper
handful of flat-leaf parsley, chopped

This is a Maggie Pannell recipe that a friend prepared for me. I loved it so much that I asked Maggie if I could include it here, as it is a fine example of Flash comfort.

1 Heat the oil in a heavy pan. Add the onion, garlic and ginger, and cook until the onions are softened and glassy.
2 Stir in the saffron, followed by the cherry tomatoes and honey.
3 When the tomatoes begin to soften, add the beans.
4 When heated through, stir in the olives, cinnamon and paprika. Season to taste and sprinkle over the chopped parsley.
5 Serve immediately.

Wheat-free Pasta with Cherry Tomato and Basil Sauce

160g wheat-free pasta (spelt, quinoa, etc)

extra virgin olive oil for drizzling (optional)

For the Cherry Tomato and Basil Sauce

1 tbsp olive oil

2 large garlic cloves, thinly sliced

500g cherry tomatoes, halved lengthways

handful of fresh basil leaves, roughly torn

sea salt and freshly ground black pepper

1/2 tsp runny honey

The pasta cooking rules are for every 100g pasta, use 1 litre of water and about 10g of salt.

1   Fill a large pot with 2 litres of water to cook the pasta, cover and bring to the boil.
2   While it heats, make the sauce: heat the oil in a large non-stick frying pan. Toss in the garlic, then just as it begins to colour, add the tomatoes, basil, salt, pepper and honey to offset the tomatoes' acidity.
3   Cook over a low heat for 8-10 minutes, until the tomatoes have broken down but not totally lost their shape.
4   While this cooks, cook the pasta: when the water is at a good rolling boil, add 1/2 tbsp of salt (a palmful) and wait for it to come back to the boil, then add the pasta, bring back to the boil again and cook it until al dente (use the times specified on the pack as a rough guide).
5   Drain the pasta and serve topped with a good spoonful of the sauce and a drizzle of extra-virgin olive oil if you like, and plenty of pepper.

Aglio Olio Peperoncino Brown Rice

- 160g short-grain brown rice
- salt
- grated Parmesan or pecorino cheese, to serve (optional)

For the Aglio Olio
Peperoncino Sauce
- about 1 tbsp extra virgin olive oil
- 8 garlic cloves, sliced
- 1/2 tsp chilli flakes or1 fresh chilli (deseeded for less heat), finely chopped
- sea salt and freshly ground black pepper
- generous handful of flat-leaf parsley, finely chopped
- finely grated zest of 1/2 lemon

For a tasty transformation of this add to the sauce a drained and finely chopped anchovy (in oil, drained), a tablespoon of lemon juice and a small handful of chopped mint.

1 Cook the rice in simmering lightly salted water until tender but still al dente – with a nutty bite. Drain well.
2 While it cooks, make the sauce: heat the oil in a large non-stick pan, add the garlic and chilli with a light sprinkling of salt. Cook over a low heat to allow the garlic to flavour the oil.
3 When the garlic is just beginning to colour and puff slightly, remove the pan from the heat – take care not to burn the garlic or it will taste bitter.
4 Add the drained rice to the pan and toss with the parsley, lemon zest and pepper. If a little dry, add a drizzle more oil.
5 Serve immediately, adding a little grated Parmesan or pecorino cheese if you like.

Note: If using par- or pre-cooked brown rice, just add the rice to the pan of sauce and heat through.

Hummus with Crumbled Feta and Pomegranate

- 1 (410g) can of chickpeas, drained and rinsed
- juice of 1 lemon
- 2 garlic cloves
- 2 tbsp tahini (optional)
- 2 tbsp olive oil
- sea salt and freshly ground black pepper
- 100g feta cheese, crumbled
- seeds from 1 pomegranate
- handful of fresh mint, chopped

If you are pushed for time, you can use a bought hummus with the same topping. Try popping a medium cooked beetroot into the blender with the other ingredients for a surprisingly delicious and pink version!

1 In a blender using the pulse button, blend the chickpeas, lemon juice, garlic, tahini and oil with about 4 tablespoons of water until smooth and creamy (you may need a little more water). Season to taste.
2 Using the back of a spoon, spread this hummus on a serving dish and sprinkle with the feta, pomegranate seeds and mint.

Dirty Quinoa

- 150g quinoa
- 200ml coconut milk
- 200ml boiling water
- 1 heaped tsp red or green Thai curry paste
- 1 lemon grass stalk, halved if fresh
- 3 kaffir lime leaves
- 50g frozen garden peas
- dash of nam pla fish sauce
- 1 tsp palm sugar or honey (or to taste – optional but delicious)

Dirty quinoa is comforting with a capital C. I like to have it runnier than in the picture – a sort of creamy, soupy spicy savoury porridge.

1 Place the quinoa in a saucepan with the coconut milk, water, curry paste, lemon grass and lime leaves, and gently simmer for 10-15 minutes, until the quinoa grains have a little white disc around them.
2 Add the peas halfway through the simmering process and season with fish sauce and palm sugar or honey, if using.
3 When most of the liquid has been absorbed, remove from the heat. I like to keep this fairly sloppy as I find it more comforting served as a sort of spicy porridge, but it can be served firmer as opposite.

Baked Seasoned Sweet Potatoes
with Matcha Guacamole

- **2 sweet potatoes, scrubbed but unpeeled**
- **any Flash Seasoning or commercial version of it (page 12)**
- **sea salt and freshly ground black pepper**
- **1 tbsp olive oil**
- **Turmeric and Chutney Finishing Yogurt (page 21)**

for the Matcha Guacamole
- **2 ripe avocados, peeled and stones removed**
- **juice of 1 lime**
- **1 tsp matcha tea**
- **1 large red chilli, deseeded and finely chopped**
- **2 tomatoes, finely chopped**
- **1 small red onion, finely chopped**
- **1 bunch of coriander, finely chopped**

This antioxidant-packed guacamole is my green and guilty pleasure. I especially love it with steamed asparagus. Also try sampling a new palate sensation by replacing the matcha with sumac.

1 Preheat the oven to 180°C (fan160°C)/350°F/gas mark 4.
2 Slice the sweet potatoes in half lengthways and sprinkle with your seasoning of choice and a little salt and pepper (unless using Chaat Masala, as this already contains salt).
3 Bake in the oven for 30 minutes until soft and oozing.
4 Meanwhile, make the guacamole: place the avocado flesh, lime juice and matcha in a blender, and blend to a smooth paste. Place this in a bowl and stir in the remaining ingredients. Season and set aside.
5 Serve the cooked sweet potatoes with a dollop each of the guacamole and the Turmeric and Chutney Finishing Yogurt.

Every beginning begins with an ending

Flash

Vegetables & Salads

This section explores the idea of vegetables dishes and salads as complete meals, to be served 'with mostly plants', or as interesting side dishes when you are entertaining.

Steamed Vegetables with Marinara Pouring Sauce

- selection of green vegetables for steaming
- 1/2 jar of bought tomato and basil (marinara) sauce
- freshly ground black pepper
- 50g feta cheese (optional)

This makes a quick and very satisfying after-work supper that is totally Flash. When choosing your sauce, get one with very simple and few ingredients, i.e. just tomatoes, basil, garlic, olive oil and seasoning. Try finishing the dish with a sprinkling of toasted omega-3 seeds. Steamed veg are also great with just a Flash Finishing Yogurt (page 21) and a few seeds.

1 Cook the vegetables in a steamer until just tender and while they steam, heat the sauce.
2 When the vegetables are cooked, put them in a bowl and pour the sauce over them.
3 Top with plenty of black pepper and a little crumbled feta, if using.

Sweet Miso Aubergine

- 1 aubergine
- olive oil
- sesame seeds, to garnish (optional)

for the Dengaku Sweet Miso Paste
- 5 tbsp miso paste (brown or barley work best)
- 2 tbsp thick set honey
- 1 tbsp sake or mirin

This is an example of Japanese comfort food at its best – wonderfully veggie but with one foot in comfort. Transform it into a complete meal with a spoonful of Matcha Finishing Yogurt (page 21).

1 First make the Dengaku Sweet Miso Paste: combine all the ingredients in a heavy-based pan and stir with a wooden spatula over a medium heat. When it begins to boil, reduce the heat and continue stirring until smooth and thickened. Leave to cool.
2 Cut the aubergine in half and, using the point of the knife, cut along the edge as close to the skin as possible – as you would a grapefruit – to loosen the flesh inside.
3 Score the loosened flesh at an angle across the top one way and then the other to form a diamond lattice pattern.
4 In a lightly oiled pan, cook the aubergine halves, flesh down, over a medium heat until golden, turn them over, cover and cook until tender.
5 Preheat the grill to high. Take the aubergine halves out of the pan, place on the grill pan and spread a tablespoon of the miso paste on top of each. Place under the grill and cook for 4-6 minutes, until the aubergine is soft, but taking care not to burn the miso paste.
6 Serve garnished with sesame seeds if you like.

Flash Glazed Cauliflower Cheese Steaks

1 large cauliflower

1 tbsp harissa paste (rose or
ordinary)

1 tbsp olive oil, plus more
for frying

sea salt and freshly ground
black pepper

75g feta cheese, crumbled

These vegetable steaks are wonderful served with Pomegranate Vinaigrette (page 23) and plenty of chopped fresh mint. The harissa glaze can be replaced with any Flash Glaze (page 13); omit the feta and serve with a Flash Finishing Yogurt (page 21) instead.

For a short cut, season the cauliflower steaks with any of the Flash Seasonings (page 12) and fry in a little olive oil. Sprinkle with a Flash Finishing Salt (page 19) and serve with any of the Finishing Yogurts (page 21) and a scattering of chopped fresh herbs.

1 Preheat the oven to 180°C (fan160°C)/350°F/gas mark 4.
2 Using a sharp knife, cut 2 thick slices of cauliflower, starting from the top centre of the head and cutting right down through the stalk. (Use what's left over for soup.)
3 Mix the harissa paste with the oil and brush this over the cauliflower steaks on both sides. Season with a little salt and pepper.
4 Fry the steaks in a lightly oiled pan until golden on both sides. Remove from the pan and place on a baking tray.
5 Brush the tops of the steaks with the remaining glaze and bake in the oven for about 10 minutes.
6 Top with cheese and return to the oven until the cauliflower is tender and the cheese has taken on some colour and is beginning to melt.

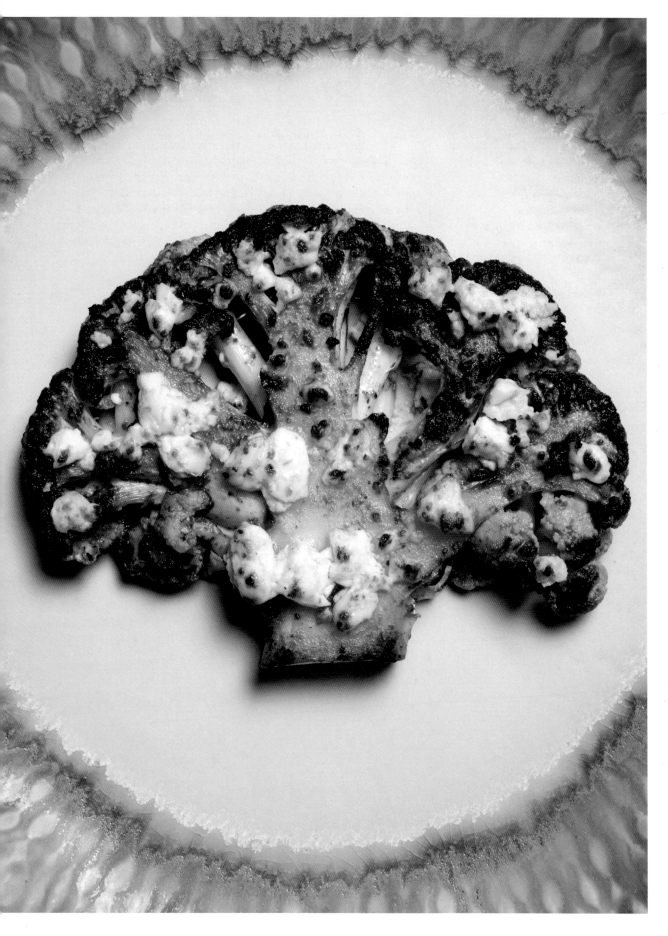

Seasoned Roasted Vegetables

- 1 red onion, cut into quarters
- 1 large carrot, cut into batons
- 1/2 aubergine, cut into chunks
- 1 large head of broccoli, separated into large florets
- 1 courgette, cut into rounds
- 1 head of garlic, top sliced off to expose the cloves
- 1 tbsp Herbes de Provence (page 12)
- sea salt and freshly ground black pepper
- 3 tbsp olive oil
- 1 1/2 tbsp thick balsamic vinegar (I use Belazu)
- 1 punnet of cherry tomatoes
- 1 red pepper, deseeded and cut into pieces
- 1 yellow pepper, deseeded and cut into pieces
- 2 Portobello mushrooms, sliced
- Red Pesto and Parsley Finishing Yogurt (page 21)
- Dried Lavender Gremolata (page 23, optional)

See the grid on page 156 for ways of varying the flavouring of and accompaniments to this simple but satisfying dish. The vegetables listed in this recipe are just to give you an idea - you can use any veg, taking into account that some cook faster than others. Transform it into a complete meal with a scattering of mixed seeds and a Finishing Yogurt (page 21) or grated goats' cheese.

1 Preheat the oven to 180°C (fan 160°C)/350°F/gas mark 4.
2 Place the onion, carrots, aubergine, broccoli, courgettes and garlic in a large ovenproof dish. Sprinkle with some of the herbs, salt and pepper, and drizzle with the olive oil and balsamic vinegar.
3 Roast in the oven for 20 minutes.
4 Add the tomatoes, peppers and mushroom. Season with more herbs and a little salt, and return to the oven for a further 10-15 minutes.
5 Serve with Red Pesto and Parsley Finishing Yogurt, and top with Lavender Gremolata.

Raw Vegetable Wraps
with Tara's Ginger and
Lime Dipping Sauce

6 rice paper discs, 23cm
(9 inches) in diameter

for the filling
- 6 Baby Gem lettuce leaves
- 1 carrot, cut into thin matchsticks
- $^{1}/_{2}$ cucumber, cut into thin matchsticks
- 1 avocado, peeled, stoned and cut into slices
- handful of alfalfa sprouts
- handful of any sprouting beans or bean shoots
- 1 red pepper, deseeded and cut into strips
- 1 yellow pepper, deseeded and cut into strips
- handful of fresh herbs, such as mint, coriander or basil

For Tara's Ginger and Lime Dipping Sauce
- juice of 2-3 limes
- 2 tbsp fish sauce
- 1 tbsp runny honey
- 1 red chilli, deseeded and finely chopped
- 1 garlic clove, finely chopped
- 1 thumb-sized piece of fresh ginger root, grated

For a more robust meal, add a little crab meat or cooked shelled prawns. You can really put whatever salad veg you like into these wraps. They are also lovely filled with fresh fruit.

1 Soak a rice paper disc in a tray of warm water for about 35 seconds until softened. Lift out and place flat on a clean tea towel to drain.
2 Place a lettuce leaf in the centre of the rice paper and fill it with a little of each vegetable and some herbs. Fold over edges of the paper and roll up to make a parcel (as the rice paper will be slightly tacky it will hold its shape).
3 Repeat with the remaining rice paper discs and filling ingredients.
4 To make the dipping sauce, combine all the ingredients in a bowl.
5 Using a sharp knife, cut each roll across in half at an angle to reveal the brightly coloured vegetables. Serve with the dipping sauce.

Sumac-roasted Tomatoes

- **6 ripe tomatoes, preferably 'on-the-vine'**
- **sea salt and freshly ground black pepper**
- **light sprinkling of molasses sugar**
- **olive oil**
- **1 tbsp sumac**
- **3 sprigs of thyme, leaves only**

I love these with thin slices of pecorino or feta cheese accompanied by a simple salad of Baby Gem lettuce leaves with an olive oil and lemon juice dressing.

1. Preheat the oven to 150°C (fan 140°C)/300°F/gas mark 2.
2. Cut the tomatoes in half and place on a baking tray. Season with salt and pepper, and add a light sprinkling of sugar. Drizzle with oil, then sprinkle with the sumac and thyme leaves.
3. Slow-roast the tomatoes until soft and beginning to caramelize, about 20-30 minutes.

Urban Belly Wrinkled Beans

- 2 tbsp sesame oil
- 2 splashes of soy sauce
- 2.5cm (1 inch) fresh ginger root, grated
- 3-4 garlic cloves, finely chopped
- 7 sun-dried tomatoes in oil, drained and finely chopped
- 1 lemon grass stalk, tough outer leaves removed and stalk cut lengthways into 4 pieces
- squeeze of Taste #5 Umami Paste or Marmite/Vegemite
- 400g fine green beans, trimmed
- 2 splashes of fish sauce
- 2 splashes of soy sauce
- furikake or toasted sesame seeds, to serve

I first had these beans in Chicago at Urban Belly, chef Bill Kim's noodle bar, a tasty temple to deliciousness. This simple gourmet experience left me with salivating memories and a pledge to return. To turn these into a complete meal, add a couple of handfuls of cashew nuts or almonds with the beans.

1 To a blender, add 1 tablespoon of the sesame oil with the soy sauce, ginger, garlic, sun-dried tomatoes, lemon grass and umami paste, then blitz until just becoming a paste.
2 Heat a wok until very hot, then add the remaining sesame oil and the blended paste, and stir-fry until fragrant. Add the beans and stir-fry until coated with the paste.
3 Add the fish sauce and soy sauce with a splash of water. As the water evaporates, add more splashes one at a time, until the beans are softened and beginning to wrinkle, but are still al dente.
4 Serve with a sprinkling of furikake or toasted sesame seeds.

Stir-fried Shredded Cabbage with Caramelized Dates and Caraway Seeds

- knob of butter
- 1 tbsp olive oil
- 1 white cabbage, cored and finely shredded
- 8 dates, stoned and finely chopped
- 1 tsp caraway seeds
- salt flakes and freshly ground black pepper

The toffee-like dates, mingling with the punchy caraway seeds, take an ordinary cabbage to buttery new heights. As you can imagine, this also works well with finely shredded red cabbage. For a complete meal, top each portion with a poached egg – surprising but delicious. Dates and eggs are traditionally served together in Persian cooking.

1 Heat the butter and oil in wok. Add the cabbage, dates and caraway seeds, and stir-fry until the cabbage is tender but still al dente. Season to taste.

Umami Broccoli with Feta and Toasted Walnuts

- **400g Tenderstem broccoli**
- **handful of walnuts**
- **Taste #5 Umami Vinaigrette (page 23)**
- **100g feta cheese, crumbled**

This is delicious served in larger quantities as a side dish at dinner parties and can be made in advance. For the record, Italians usually dress their vegetables with oil and vinegar or lemon juice rather than butter. Try dressing your vegetables like salads, with simple extra virgin olive oil, lemon juice and a little salt and pepper, or experiment with any of the Flash Dressings on page 23.

1 Steam or boil the broccoli until al dente.
2 While it is cooking, toast the walnuts in a dry frying pan until browned but not burnt.
3 Drain the broccoli and place on a serving dish. Drizzle with the Umami Vinaigrette and top with feta cheese and a sprinkling of toasted walnuts.

Carrot and Tuna Salad

- **6 large carrots, grated**
- **1 (50g) can of tuna in brine or spring water, drained**
- **1 red onion, finely chopped**
- **handful of chopped flat-leaf parsley**
- **2 tbsp olive oil**
- **squeeze of lemon juice**
- **sea salt and freshly ground black pepper**

I love this recipe and have adapted it from Harumi Kurihara's brilliant book *Harumi's Japanese Cooking*. For those of you who don't know, Harumi is Japan's answer to Delia Smith.

1 In a large bowl, combine the carrots, tuna, onion and parsley. Dress with the olive oil and lemon juice, then season.

Lentil Salad with Green Apple, Red Onion and Dill

- 250g cooked vac-pack or tinned black beluga or Puy lentils (Merchant Gourmet)
- 1 red onion, finely chopped
- 1 garlic clove, peeled and cut in half
- 2 large Granny Smith apples, diced
- 1 bunch of dill, roughly chopped
- 2-3 tbsp olive oil
- juice of 1/2 lemon juice
- sea salt and freshly ground black pepper

This colourful, tasty and satisfying salad was born from having nothing but these ingredients in the house and a very hungry unexpected guest. Now she keeps popping in on the off-chance!

1   In a large bowl, combine the lentils, onion, garlic, apple and dill. Dress with the oil and lemon juice, then season.

Other Salad Ideas

There are so many different ways to make a salad, and salad recipes to me are more notional than instructions to the letter. These are some ideas for interesting flavour-packed combinations. In each case, to make the following add the listed ingredients to a bowl of mixed leaves:

Umami Niçoise
Drained canned tuna, cooked green beans, shelled hard-boiled egg, black olives, tomatoes, etc. For the dressing, mix a squeeze of Umami Taste #5 paste or anchovy paste with 2 tablespoons of olive oil, a squeeze of lemon juice and plenty of black pepper.

Roast Chicken Salad with Sun-blushed Tomatoes and Tarragon
Skinless roast chicken, sun-blushed tomatoes, fresh tomatoes and a handful of chopped fresh tarragon. Dress with Flash Mustard Vinaigrette (page 23).

Feta and Watermelon Salad
Toss the leaves with diced feta and watermelon and a handful of toasted pumpkin seeds. Dress with Pomegranate Vinaigrette (page 23).

Baby Gem & Fennel Salad
with Prawns & Mint

- 4 **Baby Gem lettuce hearts**
- 2 **heads of fennel**
- **300g cooked king prawns**
- **1 large bunch of mint,
  roughly chopped**
- **extra virgin olive oil**
- **lemon juice**
- **sea salt and freshly ground
  black pepper**

This is one of my favourite salads and often I eat it without the prawns, as it makes a wonderful accompaniment to any Flash dish. For those of you who don't mind the breath, it is wonderful with a scattering of chopped spring onion.

1 Cut the lettuce hearts into quarters lengthways, then quarter the fennel bulb and cut into crunchy slices. Put them in a salad bowl.
2 Add the prawns and mint, and dress with the oil, lemon juice and seasoning to taste.

If you want to be heard keep it simple

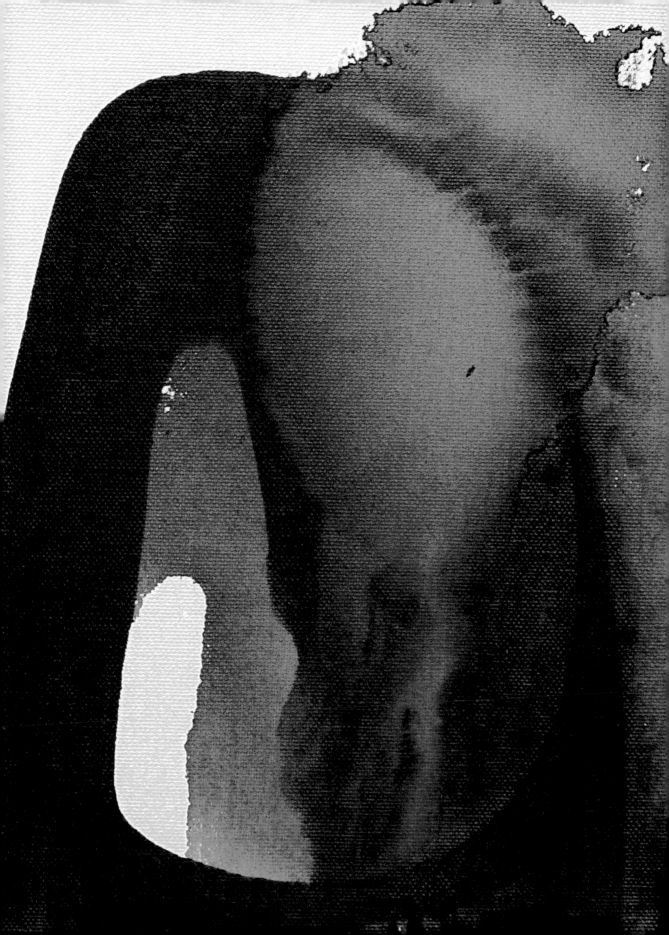

Flash

Soups

Soup is one of my favourite meals – both comforting and filling. With a spoonful of finishing yogurt and a slice of wheat-free toast or crackers, they become light but complete meals in a Flash, especially when served 'with mostly plants'. All the soups in this section serve 4.

Asparagus Soup with Peas and Mint

1 tbsp olive oil

1 onion, roughly chopped

3 garlic cloves,
roughly chopped

1 kg green asparagus, woody
ends discarded and stalks
chopped into 2.5cm
(1 inch) lengths)

250g garden peas or petit pois
(frozen is fine)

2 litres vegetable stock or
3 organic vegetable stock
cubes dissolved in that
amount of hot water

1 large handful of mint

sea salt and freshly ground
black pepper

This soup was inspired by Vivien Kay's transformational detox retreat Simply Healing. Try adding a small spoonful of Prosciutto and Parmesan Paste (page 17) on the soup for a massive umami hit, as asparagus and peas are among the few vegetables with their own umami rating.

1 Heat the oil in a heavy-based pan, add the onion and garlic, and sizzle just enough to release their flavours but not to colour them.
2 Stir in the asparagus and peas and top with enough stock to come 5cm (2 inches) above the asparagus mixture. Bring to a simmer.
3 When the asparagus stalks are soft, add the mint and seasoning, then blend to a nice soupy consistency.
4 Serve with a dollop of any of the pastes, props or finishing yogurts on pages 16-21.

Curried Sweet Potato and Ginger Soup

1 tsp olive oil

1 onion, chopped

3 garlic cloves, peeled

1 chunky thumb-sized piece of fresh ginger, grated unpeeled

1 tsp garam masala

3 large sweet potatoes, peeled and cut into chunks

2 organic vegetable stock cubes, crumbled

sea salt and freshly ground black pepper

This is delicious with Turmeric and Chutney Finishing Yogurt (page 21) and a sprinkling of chopped coriander. Alternatively, drizzle with the Finishing Yogurt and sprinkle with Coriander and Fennel Salt (page 19) and marigold petals as a Flash Entertaining vegetable accompaniment. For a sweet potato and ginger mash, add less water and mash with a knob of butter for the most delicious and comforting result.

1 Heat the oil in a large saucepan. When hot, add the onion, garlic, ginger and garam masala, and cook until the onion becomes softened and glassy.
2 Add the sweet potato with 1.5 litres of water and the stock cubes.
3 Cover and bring to the boil. When boiling, reduce the heat and simmer until the sweet potato is soft.
4 Blend using a hand blender and adjust the seasoning.

Quick Miso Monday Soup

- 1 litre good chicken stock (or 1 organic chicken stock cube crumbled into 1 litre of boiling water)
- good handful of shelled raw king prawns
- 1 thumb-sized piece of fresh ginger root, cut into slices
- 1 red chilli, thinly sliced (deseed for less heat)
- 2 garlic cloves , sliced
- 3 dried shiitake mushrooms
- 2 handfuls of mange touts
- 2 handfuls of baby spinach leaves
- 2 spring onions, cut into 2cm/3/4 inch lengths
- 2 tsp miso paste (preferably light)
- handful of coriander, chopped

This recipe can also be made by using miso paste sachets, follow the packet instructions to make up 2 portions of broth, then proceed as below. You can replace the prawns with 1 or 2 chicken breasts or 300g of tofu, chopped into cubes and any vegetables, including sea vegetables like wakame or edible seaweed flakes can be added. If you are in need of Flash Comfort you can replace the prawns or chicken with udon or brown rice noodles. Cook the noodles in plenty of simmering water until just al dente, according to package directions. Rinse them in cold water and drain, then add to the very hot soup just before serving.

1 Put the stock, prawns, ginger, chilli, garlic and shiitake mushrooms in a large saucepan.
2 Bring to the boil, then reduce the heat and simmer for 20 minutes.
3 When broth-like and no longer watery, add the mange touts, spinach and spring onion. Cook until the mange touts are tender but still al dente.
4 Remove from the heat and whisk in the miso paste and coriander.

Quick Sumac and Mint Gazpacho

- **1.5 litres tomato juice**
- **1 punnet of cherry tomatoes**
- **1 red pepper, halved and deseeded**
- **1 yellow pepper, halved and deseeded**
- **1/2 cucumber**
- **1/4 red onion**
- **2 garlic cloves**
- **2 pieces of rye crispbread**
- **good handful of ice cubes**
- **1 tbsp olive oil**
- **1 tbsp red or white wine vinegar**
- **1 tsp sumac**
- **bunch of fresh mint leaves**
- **sea salt and freshly ground black pepper**

For the ultimate liquid lunch, serve this with a few nuts in a peaceful outdoor space.

1 Place all the ingredients except the mint and seasoning in a food processor or, if using a stick blender, place in a large, suitable container. Blitz until smooth.
2 Mix in the mint and seasoning to taste.

Broccoli and Lemon Soup

- 1 unwaxed lemon
- 2 tbsp olive oil
- 4 garlic cloves, roughly chopped
- 1 leek, thinly sliced
- 1 large onion, roughly chopped
- 1kg broccoli (about 3 large heads), separated into florets
- 3 organic vegetable stock cubes, crumbled
- sea salt and freshly ground black pepper

I love this served with a dollop of Turmeric and Chutney Finishing Yogurt (page 21) or my Prosciutto and Parmesan Paste (page 17). I first had this wonderfully lemony soup at Joan's On 3rd in Los Angeles. The whole pieces of lemon zest give it a creamy quality, and at Joan's I think they might add a splash of cream. I like it really sharp and punchy, but you can add more or less zest, according to your taste.

1 Using a sharp knife, pare the zest off the lemon in long strips, top to bottom. You will end up with a 'naked' lemon and about 5-6 long strips of zest with a very thin layer of pith on the underside.
2 Heat the oil in a large saucepan. When hot, add the garlic, leek and onion, and stir until the onion begins to get glassy but not coloured.
3 Add the broccoli and stir all together. Add 2 litres of water, the stock cubes, lemon zest strips and plenty of pepper.
4 Cover and bring to the boil. When boiling, reduce the heat and leave to simmer until the broccoli is tender enough to blend with a hand blender but still nice and green. If during cooking you need to add a little more water, add a cupful or so more, remembering that you want this soup to be nice and thick, so do not dilute too much.
5 Remove from the heat and blend with a stick blender. Adjust the seasoning and add a squeeze of lemon juice if you like.

Beetroot and Watercress Borscht

1 large orange
2 tbsp olive oil
1 large red onion, chopped
3 garlic cloves
1.5 kg beetroot, peeled and coarsely diced
1 tbsp grated horseradish (bottled or fresh)
2 organic vegetarian stock cubes, crumbled
handful of fresh dill
freshly ground black pepper
2 bunches of watercress, lower stalks removed and leaves roughly chopped

To serve
low-fat crème fraîche
Dried Lavender Gremolata (page 23, optional).

This marriage of old friends is an iron bomb and tastes delicious, especially with a dollop of low-fat crème fraîche and a sprinkling of Dried Lavender Gremolata. Blending the watercress into the hot soup at the end cooks it very gently and briefly, without destroying all its nutrients and making the soup sludgy. You can do this with lots of soups, using baby spinach, watercress, rocket or just mixed herbs. The orange's vitamin C also helps the iron in the beetroot and watercress to be absorbed more readily by the body.

1 Using a sharp knife, pare the zest off the orange in long strips top to bottom. You will end up with a 'naked' orange and about 5-6 long strips of zest with a thin layer of pith on the underside.

2 Heat the oil in a large saucepan. When hot, add the onion and garlic, and sauté until the onion becomes glassy. Add the beetroot and stir, then add 2 litres of water, the horseradish, crumbled stock cubes, the orange zest and the dill. Season with pepper (you probably won't need any salt, as the stock cubes should have enough).

3 Cover and bring to the boil. When boiling, turn down the heat and simmer until the beetroot is tender enough to blend with a stick blender.

4 Remove from the heat, stir in chopped watercress with juice from the orange and blend.

5 Adjust the seasoning and serve with a dollop of low-fat crème fraîche and a sprinkling of Dried Lavender Gremolata.

We can all learn new tricks

Flash

Starters & Desserts

Entertain from the heart by picking any one of the following starters and desserts to top and tail any main course recipe for a fully Flash meal to impress. You can also pick side dishes from the Vegetable & Salads section (page 112-127). All the recipes in this section serve 4.

Starter: Avocado Vinaigrette

2 large avocados
double quantity of any of
the Flash Dressings (page 23)

This is so simple and so perfect. If you want to remove the skin and slice the avocado, you can drizzle the dressing over the slices. For something a little more substantial, add a spoonful of white crab meat; otherwise serve with toasted wheat-free sourdough bread and good quality butter – you don't have to eat it!

1 Cut the avocados in half and remove the stone. Spoon the chosen dressing into the hollow.

Starter: Iceberg Wedge with Caesar Dressing

1 Iceberg lettuce
snipped chives, to garnish

for the Caesar Dressing
3 garlic cloves, crushed
1 tbsp Dijon mustard
1 tbsp white wine vinegar
sea salt and freshly ground
black pepper
1 heaped tbsp low-fat
Hellman's mayonnaise
1 heaped tbsp low-fat
natural live yogurt
3 drained canned anchovy
fillets in oil (optional)
4 tbsp extra virgin olive oil
1 tbsp grated Parmesan cheese
dash of Worcestershire sauce
squeeze of lemon juice

1 First make the dressing: in a food processor, blend together the garlic, mustard and vinegars with a couple of pinches of salt. Add the mayonnaise, yogurt and the anchovies, if using them, and blend again. Slowly add the oil until the mixture has a thick dressing consistency. Using a spatula, fold in the Parmesan cheese, Worcestershire sauce and seasoning, and stir in the lemon juice.
2 Remove the outer leaves from the lettuce and cut it into 4 wedges.
3 Place a wedge on each plate, spoon the dressing across the middle of each wedge, leaving the points free. Garnish with snipped chives.

Starter: Asparagus with Flash Finishing Salts, Props and Yogurts

_ **16 large green asparagus spears**
_ **a Flash Finishing Salt (page 19)**
_ **a dollop of Flash Finishing Yogurt (page 21)**
_ **a Flash Prop (page 23), to garnish**

This classic starter is also wonderful with a dollop of matcha guacamole, (page 108).

1 Using a peeling knife, shave any tough skin from the bases of the asparagus stalks and trim the ends.
2 Boil or steam the asparagus until just tender.
3 Serve, hot, warm or cold with a sprinkling of Finishing Salt, a dollop of Finishing Yogurt on the side or in a little ramekin and decorate with a Prop.

Starter: Soup & Spelt

Serve any soup from the soup section (pages 130-141), decorated with a Flash Prop (page 23) of your choice. Serve with toasted spelt bread and a drizzle of olive oil. Again, you can pass on bread if you want to stay Flash.

Entertaining from the heart
Opposite (clockwise from the top left): Asparagus Soup with Peas and Mint (page 131) with Turmeric Finishing Yogurt and decorated with rose petals; Asparagus with Flash Finishing Salts, Props and Yogurts; Iceberg Wedge with Caesar Dressing (page 145); and Avocado Vinaigrette (page 145) with Pomegranate Vinaigrette (page 23) and some pomegranate seeds.

Dessert: Sorbet Swizz

- 500ml good-quality lemon sorbet
- 50g fresh basil leaves
- generous splash of Martini Bianco or vodka
- wafer or biscuit, to serve

1 Sneak away from the table and remove the sorbet from the freezer about 10 minutes before you plan to serve dessert.
2 When ready to serve, tip the sorbet into a tall container, add the basil and the splash of liquor, and blitz with a hand blender for a second or two. Take care not to blitz too much as this will make it runny rather than a nice whippy consistency.
3 Spoon into glasses and serve with a wafer or a dark chocolate mint.

Dessert: Chocolate Flaque
(posh for 'puddle')

- 300-400g best-quality dark chocolate (70% cocoa or above depending on your taste)
- handful of toasted almonds
- handful of dried cranberries (sugar-free if possible)
- 1 tsp dried rosemary needles
- 1/2 tsp sea salt flakes
- sprinkling of edible gold flakes (optional)

This recipe was given to me my friend Elizabeth, wife of Philip Wells, The Fire Poet, a man with a delicious way with words. Check out his inspirational work at www.thefirepoet.com. This is a festive version; see the grid on page 156 for chocolate to Lick the World ideas. You'll need a silicone baking tray or mould (worth investing in if you don't have one as you will be making this again and again). Try serving this with frozen grapes; simply rinse them and pop them in the freezer.

1 Break the chocolate into pieces and place in a bowl set over a pan of simmering water to melt (make sure the base does not touch the water, otherwise it can cook the chocolate).
2 When melted, pour the chocolate into or on to a silicon baking tray or mould in a thin layer (too thick and it becomes sickly).
3 Scatter with the nuts, berries and rosemary, and leave to cool.
4 When sufficiently set to take the salt without absorbing it, scatter with the salt flakes and gold flakes if your are using them, and leave to cool completely. Do not put in the fridge to speed up the process, as this will cause the chocolate to whiten in patches.
5 When set, carefully remove from mould and serve already broken into shards or with a little hammer for guests to smash it themselves.

Dessert: Grilled Pineapple with Vodka, Pink Peppercorns and Chilli

- 1 pineapple, sliced into rounds and core removed
- 1/2 tsp pink peppercorns, crushed using a pestle and mortar
- good splash of vodka
- 1 red chilli, deseeded and finely chopped

This can be prepared ahead and stored in the fridge until you are ready to serve.

1 Sprinkle the pineapple slices with the pink peppercorns.
2 Heat a griddle pan until very hot and add the pineapple slices. When the pineapple has softened and is coloured on both sides, remove from the pan and place on a warmed serving platter.
3 Douse with the vodka and sprinkle with the chopped fresh chilli to serve.

Dessert: Celia's Mixed Berries with Maple Syrup and Double Cream

- 1 punnet each of strawberries, raspberries and blueberries
- 3 tbsp maple syrup
- handful of chopped mint
- squeeze of lemon juice
- pinch of cayenne pepper
- small jug of double cream, to serve

Refuse the cream if you want to stay really Flash, but a splash will not stop you from being Flash.

1 Halve or quarter the strawberries if they are large. Mix with the berries, maple syrup, mint, lemon juice and cayenne pepper. Chill.
2 Serve with the double cream.

Flash

Breakfasts, Snacks & Juices

Everyone knows how important breakfast is, but that doesn't mean it needs to be calorie-laden or full of carbs. In this section I've given you lots of Flash ideas that are satisfying, healthful and easy.

Flash Waking

Get your liver going and your system cleansed by starting the day with a cup of hot water and lemon. Add a slice of lemon and a good squeeze of its juice to a cup of boiling water, and sip until you feel less bleary-eyed. In the winter I like to add a slice of fresh ginger as well. Do make sure you use unwaxed lemons, as you really don't want to be drinking chemical preservatives.

Spiritual Mise en Flash
First thing in the morning is a wonderful time to connect with yourself and your higher powers. The older I get, the more I believe it is actually worthwhile getting up before the others to get the heads-up on the day, and asking your higher power(s) (whatever or whoever that may be for you) for the insight and support to get through it, instead of calling upon them when things have already started to go wrong! Taking the time to communicate with yourself (see page 96) and feel grounded means that you can hit the ground running after breakfast and be less likely to come off-course during your day.

Breakfast

Just Fruit
I have tried many a breakfast solution, but the only one that really works for me is a simple fruit plate, the ultimate in Flash exit breakfasts (see page 161). I always include a banana and berries, and whatever else depends on what is around. I wash my fruit down with a pot of freshly brewed organic coffee with a splash of milk or cream. I must confess to this being the delight of my day, not least because I am usually alone, happy in the knowledge that those I love are also happily getting on with their days, leaving me feeling like the cat that got the cream, and the newspaper.

And when you crush an apple with your teeth
Say to it in your heart,
Your seeds shall live in my body,
And the buds of your tomorrow shall blossom in my heart,
And your fragrance shall be my breath,
And together we shall rejoice through all the seasons.
Kahlil Gibran

I found this lovely quote in a very special book by Deanna Minich, *Chakra Foods for Optimum Health*, which is also the inspiration behind the juicing section overleaf.

More Flash Breakfasts

Working at home, my life can be fairly sedentary. These are more substantial breakfasts which, if you are working out or physically hard, you may need. I keep them to a minimum as, contrary to popular maxims, the bigger my breakfast, the slower I get and the hungrier I am all day. That said, I am a big luncher, so you really need to find out what works for your body.

_ 2 soft-boiled eggs and Finishing Salts (page 19)
_ Egg white omelette with Taste #5 Umami Paste (page 91)
_ Porridge with banana and cinnamon

Add half a sliced banana and or blueberries and a pinch of hunger-staving cinnamon to your usual porridge.

Toasted wheat-free pumpernickel or spelt bread with honey, nut butter, sugar-free jam or Marmite.

Boost up your fruit plate by adding 1 tablespoon low-fat live Greek-style yogurt , some Omega-3 bomb, 1 teaspoon honey, and a pinch of turmeric. (Omega-3 Bomb = 1 teaspoon each pumpkin seeds, sunflower seeds and flax seeds.

Flash & Smooth: add a banana to any flash juice combination (see opposite). For a more substantial smoothie, add 1 tablespoon oats and a splash of low-fat live yogurt. If you have guests for breakfast or brunch you can impress them with your Flash skills by rustling up any of the egg recipes on pages 86-95.

Flash Snacks: 10 Fuel Ideas

Although I try very hard not to eat between meals, it is important to have some fallback solutions should you be tempted. These work for me at those 'mid' moments, either morning or afternoon, when I just cannot wait for the next meal.

Flash Tip: Always consume Flash snacks with a full glass of water.

_ 1 glass of any Flash juice combinations (see later)
_ 2 rice cakes or oatcakes
_ 7-11 almonds
_ 2 Medjool dates (be warned that these taste like sticky toffee because they are filled with sugar, albeit natural)
_ 1 apple (a day to keep the doctor away)
_ 1 carrot, cut into batons (you can mix and match these with chopped celery, cucumber and cherry tomatoes)
_ 2 squares of 70% dark chocolate (lovely with a cup of green tea at 4pm and an equally delicious replacement for cake)
_ Any of the chakra juices opposite (1 glass)
_ Small chunk of Parmesan cheese (packed with satisfying umami and calcium)

Flash Juices & Drinks

Sun and Moon Tea

I first came across this magical idea in California. Whether you believe in drinking the moon's powers or not, they certainly make for a talking point, and next time you see sun or moon tea featured, you will know what it's all about. I confess to love creating these super-charged teas packed with energetic power and flavour.

Make up your favourite herbal teas, adding extra flavourings like cinnamon, orange or lemon slices and fresh herbs. Then sit it in the light of the sun or/and the moon. Drink and feel the energy. You can also add clean crystals to these drinks for extra magical powers; for example, to rose tea add mint and lemon zest, and place a rose quartz crystal in the jug (ideal for healing hurt feelings).

To brighten up the chakras

Chakras are the body's energy points, according to ancient Indian medicine. Each point corresponds to a set of physical and emotional symptoms; by boosting the various chakra points, your bodily and spiritual balance can be optimised. Food is a key way to add or reduce the energy in these points.

This concept is ancient, but more recently nutritional/medical research has shown that the pigmentation chemicals that give fruits and vegetables their colours also provide a culinary kaleidoscope of good health. So just make sure you consume the rainbow of colourful and healing foods available to us to keep your body in tip-top balance.

These chakra juices can be taken with breakfast, or any other time in the day.

Red: Base/Root Chakra (Life)

Apples, blood oranges, cherries, cranberries, nectarines, pink grapefruit, pomegranates, raspberries, redcurrants, red pears, red plums, rhubarb, strawberries, watermelon
Beetroot, radishes, red cabbage, red chard, red chillies, red peppers, tomatoes

Orange: Sacral Chakra (Health)

Apricots, cantaloupe, clementines, kumquats, mandarin oranges, mangos, nectarines, oranges, papayas, passion fruit, peaches, persimmons, satsumas, tangerines
Carrots

Yellow: Solar Plexus Chakra (Intellect)

Bananas, grapefruit, lemons, pineapples
Yellow peppers, ginger

Green: Heart Chakra (Balance)

Avocados, grapes, honeydew melon, kiwi fruit, pears
Broccoli, Brussels sprouts, celery, chard, courgettes, cress, cucumbers, green peppers, kale, leafy greens, lettuce, rocket, Savoy cabbage, spinach, wheatgrass

Blue: Throat Chakra (Communication)
Indigo: Brow Chakra (Higher Knowledge)
Violet: Crown Chakra (Higher Consciousness)

Blackberries, blueberries, figs, plums, purple grapes, raisins
Red cabbage

Flash Transformations

Flash	Western	Middle Eastern
Fish Fillet Parcels See page 46. Add the following to 2 firm white fish fillets drizzled in olive oil and wrap in parchment paper.	¼ red onion, sliced, 2 garlic cloves, sliced; 1 tsp fennel seeds; 1 tsp dill seeds; 2 slices of lemon; 2 sprigs of parsley; sea salt & freshly ground black pepper; 30g butter	¼ red onion, sliced; 8 stoned green olives, halved; 2 pinches of sumac; 2 slices of lemon; 2 sprigs of dill; 2 pinches of ground cumin; sea salt & freshly ground black pepper; 30g butter
Stuffed Chicken Pockets See page 71. Stuff each pocket with 1 tbsp of paste (right), wrap in pancetta and glaze (right). When cooked, serve with a drizzle of dressing (right).	Stuffed Chicken Pockets with Red Pesto & Ricotta, page 71	2 tbsp Red Pepper & Orange Paste (page 17), Pomegranate Glaze (page 13), Pomegranate Vinaigrette (page 23)
Scrambled Eggs See page 95.	Top with a dollop of tapenade or red or green pesto & a sprinkling of chopped flat-leaf parsley	Top with a dollop of harissa paste and sprinkle with mint & pomegranate seeds
Brown Rice See page 102. Add 2 tsp of any Flash Seasoning (page 12) to the olive oil when frying the garlic. Top with any suggested herbs	Aglio Olio Peperoncino Brown Rice, page 102	Baharat (page 12), chopped mint
Roasted Mixed Veg See page 116. Sprinkle with Flash Seasoning (page 12), drizzle with Flash Glaze (page 13) and top with any Finishing Yogurt (page 21)	Herbes de Provence (page 12), Balsamic Glaze (page 13), Artichoke & Caper Paste (page 17)	Baharat (page 12), pomegranate molasses, Red Pepper & Orange Paste (page 17)
Chocolate Flaque (See page 149) Sprinkle the chocolate with the various suggested additions to suit the rest of the meal.	Chocolate Flaque, see page 149	Coarsely chopped pistachio nuts, dried rose petals, coarsely chopped apricots, crushed pink peppercorns

Indian	Far Eastern	Umami
Maharaja's Secret, page 46	2 garlic cloves, sliced; 5cm/2-inch piece of ginger, sliced into batons; 2 spring onions, sliced; splash of soy sauce; 2 slices of lime; 1/2 tsp sichuan peppercorns; sea salt & freshly ground black pepper; 30g butter	2 tsp Taste #5 Umami Paste; sliced cherry tomatoes; ¼ red onion, sliced; 6 black olives, halved; 2 tsp capers, 6 basil or parsley leaves; 2 slices of lemon, 30g butter
2 tbsp Tomato & Tamarind Paste (page 17), Tamarind Glaze (page 13), Mango Vinaigrette (page 23)	2 tbsp Sweet Satay Paste (page 17), Soy Glaze (page 13), Ginger Vinaigrette (page 23)	100g mozzarella cheese, 1 tbsp grated Parmesan; good squeeze of Taste #5 Umami Paste; 2 strips of prosciutto, chopped; grated zest of ½ lemon; handful of parsley, chopped; ½ tbsp chopped walnuts. Serve with Umami Taste #5 Glaze (page 23) & Finishing Yogurt (page 21)
Season the raw egg mixture with a pinch of garam masala. Top with a dollop of Turmeric & Chutney Finishing Yogurt (page 24) and sprinkle with chopped coriander.	Creamy Frying Pan Scrambled Eggs with Ikura and Matcha Green Tea, page 95	Add a spoonful of grated Parmesan to the raw egg mixture; when cooked top with a squeeze of Taste #5 Umami Paste and plenty of chopped fresh herbs
Garam Masala (page 12), chopped coriander	Five-spice Powder (page 12), chopped spring onions	Good squeeze of Taste #5 Umami Paste or 1 tbsp sun-dried tomato paste
Garam Masala (page 12), Tamarind Glaze (page 13), Tomato & Tamarind Paste (page 17)	Five-spice Powder (page 12), Soy Glaze (page 13), Sweet Satay Paste (page 17)	Drizzle with Worcestershire Sauce or Taste #5 Umami Paste Glaze (page 23), plus a sprinkling of grated Parmesan
Coarsely chopped dried mango, chilli flakes, coarsely grated or chopped pared lime zest	Toasted sesame seeds, chopped crystallised ginger, lapsang souchong tea	Replace dark chocolate with white chocolate and sprinkle with grated Parmesan cheese & crushed black peppercorns plus a pinch of lavender

Flash

You

This chapter is all about becoming leader of your universe. Flash is not about weight loss but about setting realistic goals for yourself, and arriving healthfully at a place where you can shine with confidence, having cooked your way to your optimum weight, without compromising the flavour of your life.

The image opposite makes it clear that we are all quite different. Unrealistic comparisons only set us up for self-loathing and self-sabotage, which can lead to depression and lack of self worth. The media are packed with images of unrealistic airbrushed gloss. Flash is about what things really taste like, not what they look like. Next time you look at someone in a magazine, instead of wishing for those legs, wish for world peace and legislation to label clearly any images that have been digitally enhanced. Remind yourself that your job is to look the best version of you – not of someone else.

Find the resolve to use the ideas set out in this final section to turn a flavour-packed cookbook into a useful manual that will not only help you to transform the shape of your body and improve your energy levels, it could literally improve the taste of your life.

Flash You Tips

I have found healthful weight loss and weight maintenance to be about finding a regime that fits your lifestyle. There is no point losing weight in a way that is ultimately unsustainable or damaging to your long-term health.

For Flash weight loss, see the 'Flash Weight Loss' notes within individual tips. By applying the following restraints to normal Flash eating, I was able to lose the few extra pounds I was carrying and find my Flash weight within 21 days. The time taken to reach your healthy optimum weight does, of course, depend on your starting point.

Importantly, because we are all different, it is advisable to consult your doctor before embarking on a new diet and lifestyle regime.

For me, Flash weight maintenance equates to eating 3 healthful Flash meals a day, with the 80/20 rule (see right) applying, plus regular exercise (which could be as simple as brisk walking).

It is all about how you look and feel in your clothes and in front of the mirror. Don't get hung up on the numbers – your Flash weight is that at which you feel and look good in healthful body and mind. As we grow older, that weight can alter, and that is where a Flash life can really help keep life's changes within healthful parameters.

Flash Mantra
Moderation
Motivation
Movement

Flash 80/20 Balance

Everything in life is about balance. You have to know when to let go and when to rein yourself back in. My fitness and figure improved 100% by simply applying 80% of these rules 80% of the time. Now that I have found my Flash weight, I live by my Flash rules in the week and have the weekends 'off'.

This means I enjoy whatever is going, from pizza to pudding, in the knowledge that it is all part of a balanced and healthful lifestyle. Listen to your body; you might be surprised to hear that after a big Sunday lunch and perhaps a little tea, I am usually not hungry for dinner.

Flash Weight Loss
I have found that when I am trying to lose weight it is best to keep free meals to no more than 2-3 over a weekend or week. Try not to get into that terrible bingeing mode of living today because tomorrow we diet. I think this is one of the hardest things to balance in the mind. What you need to do is tell yourself that tomorrow is not a diet but that 80/20 is actually your new way of life; there is no impending deprivation, just balance.

Think of it like spending money: if you buy an expensive jacket on Sunday you are not going to go out and spend that kind of money again on Monday, because unless you can truly afford to you will end up in debt. It is exactly the same with food: enjoy the big spend because you are most definitely worth it, but do not career irresponsibly into debt. An 80:20 balance should be achieved within a 7-day week.

The Flash Plate

We all need protein but tend to eat way too much per meal. The ideal portion size is said to be the size of the palm of your hand, a deck of cards and more recently your i-phone. Use my Flash plate on page 8 as a guide to cut your protein portions per meal down to this size, except for breakfast, when it should be no more than 75g. Fill the rest of the plate with steamed green vegetables or salad.

All the recipes in the book have been written to yield expected portions, so when you start to cut them down to what you actually need, you will find you have about one spare serving portion left over after serving two. Because your protein is good quality and flavour-packed you will not feel dissatisfied and soon get used to eating 'not too much' and 'mostly plants'.

Whatever you eat in the evening, I find it is best to eat it as early as possible, unless of course you have to. After 10pm is really too late – better to have a banana, and call it a day.

Flash Weight Loss
For 21-day Flash weight loss, I restrict flesh to leaner cuts, such as chicken or turkey breast, mince or fillet steak. All Flash Flesh recipes can be adapted to these cuts; just swap chicken thighs for breast fillets. All Flash Fish is fine for weight loss.

Avoid any Flash Comfort dishes unless as part of your 80/20 'free' meals.

Keep breakfasts flash: for example ½ a grapefruit or berries with either an egg (boiled or poached) or 75g of lean protein or 1 tablespoon of low-fat live yogurt. I personally do not believe in eating 3 high-protein meals a day, beyond the usual 21-day period of most diets, as it can be very heavy on the body's elimination system. I recommend that beyond that, the other Flash breakfasts on pages 153-4 are introduced.

Flash Exit Foods

I have been food combining for years, and in my mind there is no doubt about it: not combining protein and carbohydrate in the same meal makes for a quicker, less gassy exit. Eating fruit away from all other food groups is also another steadfast rule when food combining. The only time I bend this rule is for breakfast during Flash Weight Loss.

Unrefined Wheat & Sugar

I have changed and so, I believe, has the wheat. Forget the science; I am talking about the facts as they relate to me. When I eat wheat (refined or unrefined) I feel gassy and tired. Although I have no intolerances or clinical reasons to be wheat-intolerant, when I eat wheat with refined sugar the initial good feeling has become increasingly short-lived. So I have made a decision to exclude wheat and sugar from my diet 90% of the time and I feel so much better for it – and this is from a girl who used to wear a necklace saying 'I do anything for cake'.

Cutting down on sugar and wheat is one of the hardest things to do. I noticed that, in response, my body began to find a sugar fix in everything and soon sweet potatoes were on the menu daily, as were peas and dates. Watch the sugar- and yeast-addict in you, and if you feel you are entering a sweet potato and date fest, move on to apples, cucumber and celery – especially if trying to clean up and lose weight. In the long run only you will be able to tell how much unrefined and natural sugars your body can take without turning it to fat, or worse, reawakening the addict in you.

Flash Fats

I would hate to cook in a world without extra virgin olive oil. High in monounsaturated fats and antioxidants, I believe it to be the elixir of life. Extra virgin olive oil does, however, transform negatively at high heats, so I recommend using it cold and only cooking with any olive oil on a low to medium heat. For high-heat cooking, use a very light olive oil or a blend of olive oil with a vegetable oil that has a higher 'smoke point' (the temperature at which decomposition begins to take place). Finished dishes can then be drizzled with a little cold extra virgin olive oil. I do suggest, however, keeping total oil and butter consumption to 3-4 tablespoons per day.

Flash Weight Loss
I don't eat more than 2 medium avocados a week. Although packed with health-giving oils, I have found that they can hamper weight loss if eaten in larger quantities.

Cut your olive oil consumption to no more than 2 tablespoons a day (all Flash recipes can be adapted to reduce this) and reduce or leave out any butter until you feel you can deal with it.

Flash & Flat

The general consensus among my group of friends is that if you want to wake up with a flat tummy and go to bed feeling light and lean, say no to carbs after 4pm (although my cut-off point is usually after lunch). This simple rule will improve your libido in a FLASH! Feeling bad about your body inhibits sexual drive, so get ready to feel fabulous in and out of the bedroom!

Make sure that when you do eat carbs you don't have them with protein and that they are complex* and only a small percentage of your plate, I stick to about two i-phones-worth for a carb and mostly plants meal. (* Complex carbs are unrefined and therefore release their sugars gradually, avoiding peaks and dips in energy.) As you will probably have seen, I have included a Flash Comfort recipe selection of unrefined carbs for those times when nothing else will do (page 98).

It's Complex: how to Flash the C word

I have found that it is important to work out how many carb-laden meals your body can handle in a week. This will depend on your body type, your metabolism, age and how much exercise you are getting. In my experience it is the carbs that really make the difference, so if you are like me, you need to be careful about how much of them you eat.

Flash Scales: weigh it up and stay in control

Being a self-confessed control freak, I like to weigh myself regularly; that way I am master of my body and self-image and not the other way around. I have a friend who prefers to use a particularly unforgiving favourite pair of tailored trousers with a totally unyielding bum and waistband; when they are tight she knows it is time to cut back. We all have a weight line; take care not to cross it, as that fateful step too far can lead to self-loathing and self-imposed agoraphobia! Stay Flash by whatever means you use to monitor yourself.

Flash Exercise: when less is more

It is better to have exercised a little than never to have exercised at all. Find something simple and easy that you can do 3-4 days a week. Do not set yourself difficult and impossible goals. Go for the achievable and see how you go. For a good metabolism your body should go aerobic for 30 minutes around at least 3 times per week.

Flash Eating Out or Entertaining: a sociable eating plan

The beauty of a Flash life is that you can still enjoy eating out or entertaining at home. There are no 'I'm sorry, I am only eating cereal bars', etc. moments. When dining out, start with a salad and then follow the simple Flash rules of i-phone-sized portions of protein and eating mostly plants. For home entertaining ideas, see page 144. Set your friends and family an example without skipping meals or pushing just a lettuce leaf around.

Flash Desserts: other people's pudding

My favourite dessert is OPP (Other People's Pudding) which, like others' cigarettes, tastes so much better. A couple of spoonfuls and you are done: a fix without the fat. When dining out, order a couple of desserts for the whole table and grab a spoon.

Mise en Flash: fast flavour at your fingertips

The key to any successful restaurant is '*mise en place*', French for 'everything in place'. This means having an arsenal of prepped ingredients ready before service. Mise en Flash means taking the time to shop for, or prepare, simple transformational flavours that can be on hand to add magic to your everyday cooking.

Flash Shopping: create weekly shopping lists

Clear shopping lists, either on paper or online, will ensure that you do not waste time or money when food shopping. Sticking to a clear list will also ensure that non-Flash ingredients do not creep into your Flash week. Shop for those just before the weekend – unless you have a will of steel.

Flash Earth: shop for the future

Nature has gifted us many 'superfoods' (see overleaf); nothing is by chance; each living cell exists for a reason, all artfully designed to interact and work together for universal greater good. We should all try to respect our landlady's values and maximise our contribution.

Apply the 80:20 rule to your shopping trolley by ensuring that 80% is made up of non-processed nourishing foods that boost health and assist wellbeing. If you are ready and able to look beyond your own immediate concerns, promote the greater good by supporting sustainable farming and local produce where possible.

Flash Children: deserve a Flash future

Involve your children in Flash Cooking and enlist their help in making up flavour bombs in advance. Children love mixing and chopping, and familiarising themselves with the smells, flavours and tastes. I really delight in their enthusiastically recognising the personalities of world flavours in their meals.

However, I do believe that it is important for growing children and young adults to consume all the food groups at mealtimes. I therefore always make a dish of unrefined rice, grains, barley couscous, potatoes etc, to accompany our weekday Flash meals. They don't notice that we don't eat the carbs and all it means is that one meal fits all and that all fit into their jeans!

Please note that none of the Flash weight-loss tips are recommended for children.

Flash Healthful Flavour

Although nature's healing foods are not my area of expertise, I have included some interesting facts about a handful of flavours used in this book. I encourage you to research the powers of edible life-boosting nutrients. Flash Cooking is a good start, but for more in-depth information check out informative websites like www.nutritiondata.self.com or books like *The Food Bible* by Judith Wills.

There are too many herbs and spices with too many beneficial properties to list all of them here (but see the Global Flavouring Glossary on pages 168-172. Suffice it to say that each and every herb and spice provides a dose of nature's free medicine. From cooling coriander to cleansing cardamom and digestive fennel, in the alphabet of flavour each spice also has its own healing properties.

Chilli Peppers (Capsicums)

It is their high levels of the chemical capsaicin that give chilli peppers their heat and make them high in antioxidants and with powerful anti-cancer and anti-inflammatory effects, considered beneficial to the heart function. Chillies are also a great source of Vitamin C. On a Flash weight loss note, capsaicin is also an appetite suppressant and fat burner, boosting the rate at which fat is burned while speeding up the metabolism. Get that harissa on your plate!

Chocolate

The good news is the dark chocolate with a cocoa solids content of around 70% is rich in antioxidants, and recent studies have found it may even protect the body against cancer and heart disease. These studies are based on a modest consumption; a couple of small squares a day keeps the doctor away.

Garlic, onions, leeks and chives

These and other members of the *Allium* family are liver super-cleansers, enhancing the elimination of toxins and carcinogens, making these powerful bulbs key in helping prevent cancer. For maximum benefits, regularly eat onions and garlic raw. Chew antioxidant-packed parsley to avoid healthful halitosis.

Ginger

Like many other 'superfoods', the ginger root has been used in ancient medicine for centuries. It is especially good for the intestinal tract and for promoting release of intestinal gas. Ginger is also a great warmer, and anti-inflammatory, as well as being brilliant (and safe) for nausea during pregnancy.

Honey

Honey is one of the most powerful natural antibiotics available to man and its magical healing properties have been used for thousands of years. Honey works both in and on the body and can be eaten or used to heal wounds and burns. Recently the world's bee population has been worryingly in decline; I believe it is our responsibility to keep this precious food on the planet for future generations. You can help by checking out www.adoptahive.co.uk. Keep life sweet but look less cuddly by replacing unrefined sugars with Pooh Bear's sticky best friend.

Matcha (green tea)

Green tea is rich in flavonoids that appear to be responsible for its anti-cancer effects. One serving supplies 30mg of powerful antioxidants. Aside from the obvious health benefits, matcha is also a powerful metabolism booster. Drink the tea throughout the day to keep things ticking over, and serve it with a couple of squares of 70% dark chocolate for a teatime with a happy ending. Stop drinking tea after teatime if you are having trouble sleeping.

Miso (fermented rice, barley and or soybeans)

Miso is good for strengthening the immune system as it is packed with energy-boosting trace minerals. It is also rich in protein: a tablespoon containing 2g of protein and only 25 calories. If I have over-indulged at the weekend, I have a Miso Monday - replacing lunch and dinner with a bowl of clean lean Quick Miso Monday Soup (see page 134).

Pomegranate

This ancient fruit has long been acclaimed for its high vitamin C content and healthful antioxidant properties. More recent studies suggest that pomegranate may be beneficial in reducing heart disease and that the fruit also has antibacterial and antiviral properties. Sprinkle those jewel-like seeds for decorative healing.

Turmeric

The active ingredient in sunny turmeric is curcumin, the vital medicinal properties of which have been recognised in Indian Ayurvedic medicine for thousands of years. Nowadays we should be mindful to include this colourful yellow spice in our cooking regularly. Turmeric purifies the blood and mind, and is excellent for clearing skin conditions; it is also an immune-boosting antioxidant. Flash it into your dishes for a healthful glow.

Red Wine

Red wine (it has to be red) is high in the antioxidant resveratrol, linked to preventing heart disease by increasing 'good' cholesterol and preventing artery damage. Alcohol should not be abused and does not count as one of your five a day; it is only beneficial if drunk the way my grandmother drank it, as a medicinal glass (125-150ml) with her evening meal. For double healthful happiness, combine with a couple of squares of dark chocolate at the end of your Flash meal.

Yogurt (live)

Yogurt is another ancient and fermented 'superfood'. Live bacterial cultures have been added to milk for thousands of years, transforming ordinary milk into a longevity-boosting creamy treat packed with health-supporting nutrients and probiotic 'friendly' bacteria. It is these friendly 'live' or 'active' cultures that maintain the delicate balance of our intestine's microflora, boosting the immune system. For yogurt to be a superfood, it MUST contain 'live' or 'active' probiotics. Check labelling to be sure, and I do recommend buying organic where possible.

Choose to thrive not just survive

Glossary of Global Ingredients

Baharat is a spice mix used in the Middle East, notably in Turkish, North African, Gulf state and Iranian cuisines. Its main constituents include nutmeg, black peppercorns, coriander seeds, cumin, cloves, cinnamon, cardamom, paprika and ground dried chilli. The Turks add mint, the North Africans dried rosebuds, etc.

Bay leaves are from the bay laurel tree (*Laurus nobilis, Lauraceae*) and are used for their distinctive bittersweet flavour and fragrance, mostly in long-cooked dishes like soups, stews, braises and pâtés. Being one of the few herbs that keeps its flavour well when dried, bay is one of the French herbes de Provence mix, and a constituent of Indian garam masala and other similar spice mixes.

Braggs Liquid Aminos is a proprietary liquid protein concentrate made from soy beans and sold as a healthy unfermented gluten-free replacement for tamari and soy sauce.

Caper berries are pickled oblong semi-green fruits of the caper bush (*Capparis spinosa*) about the size of grapes. They are much milder in flavour than capers (below).

Capers are the pickled undeveloped buds of the caper bush (above). Their mustard oil content develops in the pickling process, giving them an intense sharp flavour.

Caraway is the dried fruits of the caraway plant (*Carum carvi*) and have a pleasant anise flavour that has long been used in breads and other baked goods – they are the 'seeds' in traditional 'seed cake' – as well as to flavour cheeses and liqueurs. Their distinctive warm nuttiness also finds use in dishes like casseroles and curries.

Cardamom is the dried seeds of a member of the ginger family (*Elettaria cardamomum*), and can be bought as seeds or still in their green fruit pods. The latter keep their flavour longer. Much coarser in flavour, black cardamom (Amomum subulatum), is the best known of several related species. A constituent of garam masala, cardamom is most widely used in Indian and Arab cooking for its floral lemony spiciness, but is also classic in Scandinavian bakes and pastries, having been brought home by the Vikings.

Chat masala is a sweet-sour spice mixture used in the cooking of the Indian subcontinent. Its most usual constituents include amchoor (dried mango powder), dried pomegranate seeds, cumin, kala namak (Indian volcanic black salt), dried ginger, black pepper, asafoetida and chilli powder. It can also contain ajowan seeds, dried mint and/or some of the other common spice mix, garam masala.

Chervil, a relative of parsley, is a delicate herb with some of its cousin's flavour combined with a hint of anise. Common in French cuisine, it is one of their fines herbes and herbes de Provence, and often referred to as 'gourmet's parsley'. It is mostly used raw in salads and dressings for vegetables as it loses most of its flavour when cooked.

Chillies are fruits of a genus of flowering plants called capsicums, members of the nightshade family, originally from South America. Valued for their spicy heat and strong flavours, they have been farmed for at least 7,000 years. The fruits are harvested unripe and green or when ripe, when they may be red, orange, yellow or even purple. They are used fresh, pickled and dried or in crushed, flaked or powdered form. The heat is due to a chemical called capsaicin, mostly contained in the membrane around the seeds. Sweet peppers are strains of capsicum that evolved without capsaicin. Capsaicin

is a natural painkiller and also a potent anti-inflammatory and antioxidant, and may lower the risk of cancer.

Chinese five-spice powder is a ground mixture of spices used to flavour meat and poultry throughout South China and Vietnam. It usually consists of star anise, fagara (also known as Sichuan pepper), cinnamon or cassia, fennel seeds and cloves. Versions can also contain cardamom, dried ginger and liquorice root, but in most mixes the predominant flavour is star anise.

Chinese rice vinegar is made from rice or rice wine, and there are three main types. The most commonly available in the West is black rice vinegar made from glutinous (sticky) rice, which is sweet and smoky. The best are produced in the province of Chinkiang. There are also white varieties, which are more like Western vinegars, and red vinegars made from fermented red yeast rice, which are sweet, tart and salty at the same time. As well as being potent flavourings they make good dipping sauces.

Chives, part of the onion family, are like very small spring onions with much smaller bulbs at their base, which are seldom used. Their onion flavour is mild and sweet, making them an excellent last-minute addition or garnish. If being added to a cooked dish, do this at the last minute as they lose flavour and texture rapidly when heated. Chives are one of the French 'fines herbes'.

Chocolate is made from cocoa beans, the seeds of the cacao tree. Native to Central and South America, there are over 30 varieties grown and the first step in manufacture is blending different types for a particular flavour. Chocolate is labelled with its percentage content of 'cocoa solids', meaning how much is made from products of the bean. As well as for better flavour, chocolate for cooking should have a very high cocoa butter content of about 70% to improve its ability to flow and coat items. Chocolate must be melted very gently, ideally in a bain-marie or a microwave at a low setting. If it gets too hot (over 44°C/111°F), it 'seizes', becomes hard and grainy, and loses its flavour.

Cinnamon is derived from the dried aromatic inner bark of a member of the laurel family (*Cinnamomum zeylanicum*) native to Sri Lanka, but it is now grown in many tropical regions. When it is removed from the plant it is cut and rolled into the familiar 'quills'. These are a much better buy than the ground powder, which loses the warm aromatic sweetness of the spice very quickly and often contains a high proportion of related, less subtle, cassia. Cinnamon's warmth quickly made it very popular in baking, as did its affinity with fruit, especially apples. In the Middle East it is used in meat dishes like stews and tajines, and it is a vital constituent of the Indian spice mix garam masala.

Cloves are the dried aromatic flower buds of a tropical evergreen in the Myrtle family native to China, picked just before they are due to open and then sun-dried. The plants are now widely cultivated in the tropics. Valued for thousands of years for their warm, pungent spicy aroma and flavour, they are sold whole, with the flower head on a stub of stalk (an often referred to as 'nails' after their shape) or in powdered form, which loses its strength rapidly. Good fresh whole cloves should exude a little of their oil when pressed. Their warmth has been used in baking, both sweet as in spiced breads and savoury as in hams. Cloves feature in many Indian masalas. They are also used in teas and in mulled wines.

Coconut milk should not to be confused with the juice found in the centre of coconuts, but is made by pouring boiling water over grated coconut flesh, letting it stand and cool slightly and then squeezing the flesh. Left to stand, it separates out into coconut milk with coconut cream on the top. Both are used in Southern Indian, Southeast Asian and West Indian curries and stews, etc. In the West they are generally available in cans or frozen. If buying coconuts to make your own milk or cream, make sure they feel heavy and have juice sloshing around inside them; if not, they are past their best. Many people worry about coconut products as they are among the few plant-based foods high in saturated fats, but half of these are in the form of lauric acid, which actually increases 'good' cholesterol at the expense of the 'bad' better than any other fat, saturated or unsaturated.

Coriander (*Coriandrum sativum*), also known as Chinese, Japanese or Mexican parsley, is a member of the carrot family. The roots, stalks, leaves and dried seeds are all used as flavourings. Confusingly, in the USA the seeds are known as coriander, while the other parts are called cilantro. Originally from the Mediterranean region, it is one flavouring that bucked the trend and found great favour when crossing to the Americas and Asia. The zesty, orangey, parsley-like flavour of the herb divides people like few others – they either hate it intensely or can't get enough. As it has a cooling effect and goes well with the flavour of green chillies, it has become indispensable in lots of South American, Indian and Southeast Asian cooking. It can be difficult to tell it apart visually from flat-leaf parsley but its distinctive aroma soon identifies it, and in markets it is usually sold complete with its roots, which can be used in long-cooked dishes, especially in Thai cooking. The flavour of the seeds is quite different, with more of the orange to it, and has long been used in Europe, especially in baking and pickling. The seeds also feature in *à la grecque* dishes and in Indian masala mixtures. Coriander is known for being anti-diabetic, anti-inflammatory and increasing 'good' cholesterol; and the leaves have anti-microbial and anti-bacterial properties.

Cumin is very similar to caraway and often confused with it. It is the dried seeds of the plant *Cuminum cyminum*, which originated in the Eastern Mediterranean region. Strongly aromatic and spicy, cumin seeds and powder feature in most Indian spice mixtures and are essential in dhals. Surprisingly it is also used in many Mexican dishes, especially those with beans, and even appears in some Texan recipes for chili con carne. Black cumin seeds are from an unrelated plant, the nutmeg flower (*Nigeria sativa*) and are mostly used in the cooking of the northern parts of India, where it is known as *kala zeera*, and in Iran.

Curry leaves come from a plant in the citrus family (*Murray koenigii*) native to southern Asia, and which grows wild in many places, especially in the foothills of the Himalayas. It is an essential ingredient in the food of most of South India and features in Malay and Indonesian cooking. The leaves really need to be fresh to have their full distinctive aroma and flavour; so many Indians grow the plant in their gardens. It is also wise when buying fresh leaves – which are now increasingly sold in the West – to sniff them, as even some fresh leaves can have lost their aroma – and thus most of their flavour – in transit.

Curry pastes and powders abound and many are very useful, although some are far from authentic. Curry pastes have the advantage that the spices in them have already been cooked to heighten their flavours and then aged for these to develop even further. Curry powders are, in fact, very much a Western invention, although even modern India has taken to the idea. Powders have the disadvantage of quickly losing their intensity of flavour. Moreover, pastes or powders very generally labelled 'curry' are made to suit a wide range of dishes and thus actually delivering none particularly well. It is wise to try to find a paste or powder suited to the dish(es) you want to cook, e.g. tandoori, vindaloo, dhansack, etc., or make your own. Mix the curry paste into the onions as you begin cooking the dish. See also Thai Curry Pastes.

Dill is a feathery fennel-like plant (*Anethum graveolens*) of the parsley family, native to the Far East, but now grown all over the Mediterranean region and in other parts of Europe. Caraway-like, tangy and grassy in flavour, the leaves are popular in the cooking of Scandinavia, Central and Eastern Europe. Perhaps from the dill used in curing salmon as gravlax and its accompanying mustard sauce, recently it has become a widely popular herb to accompany fish. The seeds are used in pickling, notably in the pickled cucumbers known as dill pickles in the USA.

Fennel (*Foeniculum vulgare*) is another feathery-leaved member of the parsley family. There are two varieties of it used as herbs, bitter fennel and sweet fennel; the latter has a distinctly anise/liquorice flavour, while the former is more celery-like. The herb featured in the cooking in Ancient Rome and today remains popular in Italian cooking. The seeds also give their characteristic flavour to many types of Italian sausage and salami. Leaf and seeds are often paired with fish. The seeds are one the constituents of Chinese five-spice powder and some Indian spice mixes. Fennel is a strong diuretic and anti-spasmodic, and also accelerates the digestion of fatty foods, so is often seen as a slimming aid.

Fish sauce is an essential flavouring in Southeast Asia. Made by fermenting small fish in brine, straining off the liquid and allowing it to mature in the sun, it is called *nam pla* in Thailand and *nuoc mam* in Vietnam. The final composition of the sauce and its effect are broadly similar to that of soy sauce, heightening other flavours, and it is used in very much the same way.

Five-spice Powder, see Chinese Five-spice Powder

Furikake is a Japanese condiment usually used sprinkled over rice. It can vary in composition, but is generally a mixture of ground dried fish, sesame seeds, chopped seaweed, sugar, salt and monosodium glutamate. Other ingredients can include *katsuobushi* (dried fermented bonito tuna), or *okaka* (bonito flakes soaked in soy sauce and dried), salmon, shiso (Japanese mint) and dried miso.

Garam masala (meaning 'hot mixture') is probably the most common spice mix used in Northern India. Although, its constituents and their proportions vary from region to region, basically it consists of bay leaves, cinnamon, cumin seeds, coriander seeds, green or black cardamom seeds, mace, cloves and black peppercorns. These are dry-roasted and usually ground to a powder. Spicy and pungent, it goes particularly well with meat and poultry.

Gold is non-toxic and has been used in food and drink for centuries, as in the liqueur Goldwasser and *vark*, the decoration on several Indian desserts. Gold leaf sheets, flakes and dust are widely available in better baking supply outlets and online. Make sure the gold you buy is declared 'food safe standard' rather than that sold in art shops as it important that the blend of gold and oils used to roll it are also edible.

Harissa paste is a fiery North African chilli sauce, the main ingredients of which include chillies, garlic, coriander, caraway, cumin and crushed dried mint, mixed to a paste with vegetable or olive oil. Most closely linked with Tunisian, Algerian and Moroccan cooking, its exact contents vary from region to region. An ingredient in tajines, it is also used as a rub for meat and poultry, and as a table condiment.

Herbes de Provence is the name for a mixture of dried herbs typical of French Provençal cooking. Recipes vary, but thyme, bay, savory, rosemary and basil are the most usual ingredients. Mint, marjoram, fennel and tarragon may also be included in the mixture. The flavour of this mixture suits the many meat, poultry, game and vegetable dishes of Southeast France.

Horseradish (*Armoracia rusticana*) is a plant in the Brassica family, like mustard and cabbage. Native to Eastern Europe and Western Asia, its roots are rich in a compound called sinigrin which, when the root is cut or grated, is broken down into mustard oil, giving it a hot and biting flavour that is also strangely refreshing. It loses this rapidly, so needs to be used as soon as the root is cut, or the grated root needs to be pickled in vinegar. It also becomes bitter with keeping, as it does when cooked. Apart from its widespread use as a condiment with cooked beef, it also works well with oily fish and is de rigueur in the recovery cocktail Bloody Mary. Look for roots that are firm and with no sprouting and no greenish tinge, which may indicate bitterness.

Imli, see Tamarind Paste

Jasmine tea is green or white tea China tea infused with fresh jasmine flowers, so is rich in healthful antioxidants. It is used to flavour rice and in sweet dishes, especially jellies, ices and sorbets and chocolate desserts.

Juniper berries are the mature fruit of a coniferous bush of the cypress family *Juniperus communis*, found wild all over Europe, North America and the Himalayas. The berries are mostly used crushed in marinades for meat, especially game, and in pâtés. With allspice and pepper, they are used to make spiced beef. They are also the main flavouring ingredient in gin, which is very much the flavour they impart to food. Juniper is used by herbalists for infections of the urinary tract and bladder, and as an anti-inflammatory. However, as it contains a potent volatile essential oil, oil of Sabinal, taken in excess it can cause renal damage, so those with kidney disorders or who are pregnant should avoid food or drink using it.

Kaffir (or makrut) lime leaves come from the kaffir (makrut) lime tree (*Citrus hystrix*), native to Southeast Asia. They are the region's equivalent of bay leaves, being widely used in all sort of dishes, fresh and dried, to impart a lemon verbena-like flavour. Its juice and rind are used in Thai curry pastes.

Lapsang souchong tea, from the Fujian province of China, has a powerfully smoky flavour due to the withering of the tea leaves over cypress or pine wood fires. This makes it perfect for adding a hint of smoke to any dish and it makes a great rub for meat or ground into burgers. Vegetarians find it useful for providing the savoury and umami qualities of meat in meat-free dishes.

Lavender (*Lavanda officinalis*), a relative of mint, is a plant that grows wild throughout much of the Mediterranean region. Its name betrays its use by the Ancient Romans to perfume their bath water. Both flowers and leaves are used, and often added to salads or fruit dishes for their colour as well as flavour. Fresh and dried, they also feature in baked dishes. It is important to use lavender with caution as the flavour can be overpowering.

Lemons are among the most common flavouring in cooking; their pleasant mellow acidity indispensable in fish and fruit dishes, as well as in salad dressings, etc. In the Middle East, lemons are preserved in a brine/lemon juice mix, sometimes flavoured with the likes of cinnamon, garlic, cloves and bay leaves. Intensely lemony, they are used in stews and sauces as well as making a tasty condiment. Indian cooks also pickle lemons (*nimbu achar*), but with spicier flavourings like cumin, fenugreek and turmeric.

Lemon grass can be one of several species of grass native to Southeast Asia (*Cymbopogon citratus*) with a light floral aroma and lemon/limey flavour due to their citrus oil content. It is widely used in the cooking of the area, only the lower part of the stalks being used, in soups and stews. Apart from its tender inner core, Even the freshest stalks remains fibrous when cooked, so the outer layers are often removed before serving. Strips of the grass are available dried but these have little of the full flavour of the fresh stalks. Ground lemon grass, usually known by its Indonesian name, *sereh* is also available, but its flavour tends to be quite coarse so it should be used cautiously.

Liquid Aminos, see Braggs Liquid Aminos

Marigold petals, from the pot marigold variety (*Calendula officinalis*), are edible and are used fresh and dried to add colour and a citrusy flavour to food, especially salads, since ancient times. They are also often used as a cheaper substitute for saffron.

Marjoram (*Origanum majorana*), as its horticultural name implies, is closely related to oregano, but sweeter, thyme-like and more delicate. It is mostly used in fresh meat dishes, sausages and stuffings, in tomato sauces and dishes, soups, salads and egg dishes. It is considered to have a good antioxidant content and to be an antifungal.

Matcha is finely ground Japanese green tea (therefore is rich in antioxidants), used to flavour some soba noodles, green tea ice cream and confectionery. In the USA it is popular in lattes, milkshakes and smoothies, and commercial food industries use it a great deal in desserts, confectionery and biscuits.

Mint is found all over the world, due both to its sturdy and aggressive growing characteristics and because of its popularity from time immemorial. The two main varieties are spearmint (*Mentha viridis* and *M. spicata*) and peppermint (*M. piperita*). The latter contains more flavouring oils as well as menthol, which gives it its characteristic mouth-cooling effect. Their flavours find a wide range of uses in food, from sauces and jellies for meats like lamb to vegetable dishes, fruit salads, teas and baking (spearmint is normally used for these purposes, while peppermint is mostly in confectionery, ice creams and liqueurs). The fresh leaves have much more and truer flavour, but dried leaves are available. Spearmint aids digestion, is antifungal and a good source of antioxidants.

Mirin is a syrupy sweetened and fermented Japanese rice wine used as a flavouring and condiment. It often finds itself in combination with soy sauce and other flavourings for noodle dishes and marinades, such as teriyaki and yakitori. It adds a sweet, rich flavour to meats when used as a marinade or glaze. Mirin is also used in soups, stews, vegetable dishes and sauces.

Miso is a traditional Japanese seasoning in the form of a thick paste produced by fermenting soy beans, rice or barley with salt and the fungus *kojikin* (*aspergillus oryzae*). It is used for sauces and spreads, as well as in pickling vegetables or meats, and mixing with dashi soup stock for miso soup. Miso is rich in protein, vitamins and minerals. Dengaku miso is sweetened with sugar and mixed with mirin (Japanese rice wine) and sake, then used to glaze grilled foods that are then grilled again to caramelize the glaze.

Mace, see Nutmeg

Molasses sugar is another term for Muscovado or Barbados sugar, a coarser, stickier type of brown sugar nutritionally richer than other brown or refined sugars, as it retains most of the nutrients in the sugar cane as well having a fuller flavour.

Nam Pla, see Fish Sauce

Nutmegs are the dried seeds from the apricot-like fruit of a tree in the myrtle family (*Myristica fragrans*), native to the Moluccas. When the seeds are harvested, the aril, or reddish net-like covering around the husk, is separated off and both are dried. The dried aril is the spice known as mace and is sold whole as 'blades' of mace or more commonly ground to a powder. The dried husks are what we know as nutmegs. Both have a warm pervasive, aromatic flavour; that of mace is more refined than that of nutmeg, but also more pungent. Mace is mostly used in pickles and preserves – it is the flavouring in potted shrimp, for instance – as well as in mulled wine. It is also often paired with cherries and chocolate, used in the making of doughnuts and in baking. In the West, nutmeg is mostly used in sweet dishes, like puddings and custards, while Middle Eastern cooks use it with mutton and lamb and it is in many Indian spice mixes like garam masala. It is a feature of the classic béchamel sauce, the basis of so many other sauces, and northern Europe it is used with vegetables like potatoes and spinach.

Olive oil is one of the healthiest of oils as it contains no cholesterol itself and is around 75% monounsaturated fats, which lower 'bad' blood cholesterol levels and increase the 'good'. It is also rich in valuable anti-oxidants not found in other oils. However, nutritionists recommend that extra-virgin olive oil should be reserved for use cold to dress food as, being unrefined, particles in it burn at about the same temperature as butter, producing unhealthy compounds. For cooking, use ordinary refined olive oil, which doesn't burn until above pan-frying and sautéing temperatures. For deep-frying, use refined sunflower or groundnut oil, which can withstand the higher temperatures.

Oregano (*Origanum vulgare*), a close relation of marjoram (it has been called 'wild marjoram') and basil, has a much more aromatic, pungent flavour than its cousin. A real advantage it has over these relatives is that it keeps its flavour well when dried; indeed it generally becomes more powerful and rounded. Often termed the 'pizza herb', it is widely used in the cooking of Italy, Spain and other Mediterranean countries, especially Greece and Turkey, as well as South America. In many of these places it is also used as a condiment. It is used to flavour a wide range of foods, but is perhaps enjoyed at its best in tomato dishes and sauces, in tandem with fresh basil.

Palm sugar is also commonly called jaggery in parts of India and is derived from the sap of the Palmyra palm tree, which also gives us sago. Sold in cake-like form or as a buttery spread, it has an aromatic winey fragrance and flavour, which is favoured in confectionery and sweet drinks, as well as in vegetarian curries.

Paprika is made by grinding dried sweet and chilli peppers to a powder and used in many cuisines to add colour and flavour to dishes. Depending on the mix and types of peppers used, and whether or not the inner seeds and membranes are removed, paprika can range from mild to fairly hot, and varies in flavour from country to country. It is important in the cooking of Hungary (notably in goulash and paprikash) and Spain. There are three types of Spanish paprika: mild (*pimentón dulce*), moderately spicy (*pimentón agridulce*) and very spicy (*pimentón picante*), all of which are used to flavour various types of chorizo sausage. Some Spanish paprika is dried by smoking over oak, giving it a smoky flavour, and it is this that flavours the best paellas.

Peppercorns can be black, green, pink or Sichuan. Black peppercorns are the fermented sun-dried berries of the climbing vine *Piper nigrum*, grown throughout the tropics to satisfy the appetite for its hot pungent, biting flavour. Possibly the most valuable spice of all, it was at one time even used as a currency and is probably the most used addition to food after water and salt. White pepper is made from the same berries, but left on the tree for a little longer and then soaked after harvesting to separate the outer parts and get to the white seeds inside. Its flavour is hotter but much less subtle than black and is mostly used to avoid speckling white dishes and sauces, etc. with black pepper.
Green peppercorns are the unripe seeds of the same vine preserved in vinegar or brine rather than dried, and have a fresh pungent flavour that has a hint of cloves. They are mostly used in sauces and in terrines, as well as with grilled meat and fish dishes. Pink peppercorns are from a totally different plant, the Peruvian pepper tree or baies rose (*Schinus molle*) and have very little heat but instead give a sweet fruity and citrusy flavour with a resinous background.
Sichuan peppercorns or fagara are the reddish-brown dried berries of a Chinese variety of prickly ash tree and among the most ancient of Chinese spices. Their spicy woodiness is used to season meat and poultry, especially Sichuan crispy duck, and it is one of the constituents of Chinese five-spice powder.

Pomegranate molasses or syrup is made by boiling down the juice of a tart variety of the fruit to a fragrant thick dark brown liquid. Its sweet tanginess is used as a souring agent in Middle Eastern cooking, particularly in Lebanon and Iran, notably in the latter's celebrated poultry stew fesenjan. It is popular as a glaze for lamb and pork, as well as in dressings for rice and salads, and as a constituent of grenadine, the syrup used in cocktails. Many of the healthful properties attributed to pomegranates themselves seem to be held in the molasses.

Preserved Lemons, see Lemons

Rice Vinegar, see Chinese Rice Vinegar

Rose petals are dried for culinary use, as in rose petal jam. They are also popular in Middle Eastern food such as the Moroccan spice blend *ras al hanout* and in Iranian *advieh*, the spice mixture used in preparation of meat, poultry and bean dishes. Rose petals are also used for sweet dishes such as ice cream, sweet pastries and as a cordial. They may also be sprinkled whole or ground on rice and salads.

Rosemary is a hardy evergreen shrub (*Rosmarinus officinalis*) of the mint family native to the Mediterranean region, where it is one of the most common plants growing wild near the sea. Its leaves are like tiny pine needles and contain oil of camphor, giving them a strong odour and a pungent lemon/lavender/pine flavour. The herb is a mainstay of Italian cooking, and used there with roast and barbecued meats, especially lamb, in breads, in the smoking of meats and in sausages, even in sweet dishes like jams, fruit salads and compotes. Rosemary contains carnosic acid, which is thought may lower the risk of strokes and neuro-degenerative diseases like Alzheimer's, as well as an anti-cancer agent.

Saffron is the dried stigmas of the saffron crocus (*Crocus sativus*) native to Southwest Asia and used both as a seasoning and colouring agent. Famously still the world's most expensive spice by weight (it takes over 4,000 hand-picked flowers to yield an ounce), fortunately its distinctive penetrating aromatic flavour means it should be used sparingly as too much can overpower a dish. Widely used in Middle Eastern, Persian and Indian cooking, Mediterranean fish soups and Spanish paella, it also appears in many traditional breads and cakes.

Savory is a species of herb plants native to Southern Europe and the Mediterranean region, two types of which are used as herbs: summer savory (*Satureja hortensis*) and winter savory (*S. montana*), the latter generally held to be inferior. Their flavour is thyme-like but rather peppery and biting, so it needs to be used with caution. It is very popular in the cooking of continental Europe, where it is regarded as 'the bean herb' as it brings out the flavours of beans, peas and lentils. It is also popular with meat and poultry, soups, eggs and salads.

Sesame (*Sesamum indicum*) is a flowering plant cultivated for its edible seeds, which grow in pods, and widely naturalized in tropical regions. According to the variety, the seeds may be cream, brown, red, yellow and even black, the darker seeds being thought to have the best flavour. The pleasant nuttiness of the seeds is accentuated by their being toasted. Western use of sesame seeds is mainly restricted to bread, biscuits and pastries, but they get much more imaginative use in the Middle East, Asia and South America in both sweet and savoury dishes. The sesame paste, tahini, is a mainstay of Arab food (see below). Japanese cuisine makes particular use of the seeds, with tofu, in coatings, dressings and sauces, and mixed with salt as a condiment (see Furikake).

Sesame oil, expressed from the seeds, is also widely used in South Indian and Asian cooking, generally made from lightly toasted seeds and so more deeply golden in colour. The lighter oil from untoasted seeds has a very high smoke point so it popular for deep-frying. Sesame is rich in Vitamin E, which is an antioxidant and is thought to reduce blood cholesterol. It is also a laxative and helps lower blood pressure.

Shiso is the Japanese name for perilla (*Perilla frutescens*), a herb that is a member of the mint family and is also known as purple mint or Japanese basil. Its leaves look a little like round nettle leaves and there are both green-leafed and purple-leafed varieties, both of which have a minty/fennel taste. It is used both as a flavouring, especially with beans such as edamame, and as a salad leaf and garnish. Considered rich in minerals and vitamins, it also has anti-inflammatory properties and is thought to help preserve and sterilize other foods.

Sichuan peppercorns, see Peppercorns

Soy sauce (*shoyu* in Japanese) is a condiment produced by fermenting soya beans with water and salt, sometimes with an added grain, usually wheat. Its first recorded use was in China almost 3,000 years ago, and later introduced to Japan by Buddhist monks in the 7th century. It is a traditional ingredient in East and Southeast Asian cuisines, both in cooking and as a condiment. It has, however, been available in Britain for over 300 years and is reputed to be an ingredient in Worcestershire sauce. Due to soy sauce's content of free glutamates, it has a distinct basic taste called umami ('pleasant savoury taste') in Japanese (see page 00).

Star anise, also known as star aniseed or Chinese star anise, is the dried star-shaped seed pod of an evergreen tree in the magnolia family (*Illicium verum*). One of the few spices used in Chinese cooking, it closely resembles anise in flavour as it contains the same compound anethole. Sweet and with a hint of liquorice, the Chinese use it in poultry and pork dishes and the Vietnamese in their soup, pho. It is one of the principal ingredients of Chinese Five-spice powder and is used in the making of liqueurs such as pastis and anisette.

Sumac is made from the dried brick-red berries of a plant (*Rhus coriaria*) that grows wild throughout the Middle East and which have a pleasantly sour flavour. Usually crushed or ground, it is used in fish dishes, salads, kebabs and cooking lentils. The popular aromatic Arab condiment *Za'atar* mixes dried herbs with sumac and toasted sesame seeds. This is often mixed with olive oil to make a dip or spread.

Tabasco sauce is a world-famous hot chilli sauce made by the McIlhenny family since Civil War times from a variety of red chilli called tabasco, originally from Mexico, mixed with spirit vinegar and salt. Matured in white oak barrels for a minimum of 3 years, it has a characteristic flavour that is essential in Bloody Marys and a favourite dressing for seafood, especially oysters.

Tahini paste, made from pounded lightly toasted sesame seeds is popular in the Arab world and the major component of hummus bi tahini (chickpeas with tahini) and other Middle Eastern foods. Sold fresh or dehydrated, its rich nuttiness has a wide range of uses, from replacing butter in sandwiches to a dip for crudités, in sauces for falafel and vegetables, and in the widely popular aubergine dish baba ganoush.

Tamarind is the pulp around the seeds of the tamarind or Indian date tree (*Tamarindus indica*). Fresh and tender, the pulp tastes like a mixture of apricot and date, and is eaten as it is or cooked with fish or rice. Dried, it is used as a souring agent after being soaked in water. The reconstituted spicy pulp is used to add a sour fruity taste to seasoning mixes, marinades, soups, curries, chutneys and refreshing drinks. Tamarind paste, available in bottles or tins, either concentrated or more liquid, is a convenient way of using it.

Tapenade is a rich thick Provençal paste made from olives, capers, anchovies, olive oil and lemon juice. It can be made with green or black olives, so may have either colour, the black being earthier in flavour. Garlic, herbs such as basil, mustard and even brandy may also be added. In the south of France it is generally eaten as an hors d'œuvre, spread on bread or with crudités. It is also used to as a stuffing for fish or poultry fillets, and even works with lamb.

Tarragon is the leaves of a plant native to Siberia and Mongolia, and is one of the few great culinary herbs unknown in ancient times. The original wild plant, known as Russian tarragon (*Artemisia dracunculus*), has a very coarse flavour, but a cultivated variety of the plant now known as French tarragon (*A. dracunculus var sativa*) started to appear in French and Italian cooking in the late medieval period, and its intriguing aromatic sweet but slightly bitter flavour quickly established it all over Europe. It is most often used with chicken, but can be used with fish and vegetables, and in salads, dressings and sauces. The French use it to flavour their *vinegar à l'estragon*.

Taste #5 Umami Paste is the world's first umami paste, one of my internationally available range of scratch or Flash cooking tools, part of the Laura Santtini Spellbinding Flavours range. Rich, deep and intensely savoury, it blends together a number of foods rich in umami: tomato, garlic, anchovy paste, black olives, porcini mushrooms, Parmesan cheese, olive oil and just a touch of sugar and salt. Squeeze it into sauces, gravies and risottos to add depth of flavour. I add it to pastas, soups and stews, and smear it on fish, meat or vegetables.

Teriyaki sauce is basically a mixture of soy sauce, mirin and sugar, and is used by the Japanese to marinate meat, fish or poultry and/or to brush them after grilling, and then grill further to produce a tasty lacquer-like glaze. Popular in barbecues, it may also be used as a dipping sauce. Some versions of the sauce can include sake and ginger.

Thai curry pastes are blends of ground herbs and /or spices and other seasonings. Red curry paste includes red chilli peppers (fresh or dried), shallots, garlic, galangal, lemon grass, coriander roots and roasted seeds, roasted peppercorns, salt, shrimp paste and kaffir lime leaf and/or rind. Green curry paste ingredients are much the same but the chillies used are red. Yellow curry paste is also similar but includes turmeric to give it the yellow colour, and occasionally yellow chillies. To make an authentic Thai curry, most pastes need the addition of coconut milk or cream. See also Curry Pastes.

Thyme, another member of the mint family, is arguably the most used herb in European and Middle Eastern cooking. The type generally used in cooking is Garden thyme (Thymus vulgaris) but there are over a hundred others, all with slightly different flavours, including several types of lemon thyme, orange thyme and caraway thyme. It is at its best with vegetables, poultry and fatty meats, and suits long slow cooking methods such as stewing and braising. Fairly strong in flavour, it can easily overpower other flavours, so is best used with discretion. Like bay it keeps its flavour well when dried. It is one of the essential ingredients in Herbes de Provence and bouquet garnis.

Turmeric (Curcuma longa) is from a perennial plant of the ginger family native to tropical South. The plant's rhizomes are boiled for several hours and then oven-dried and ground into a deep orange-yellow powder. It is used in most curries and curry mixes/pastes, and other South Asian and Middle Eastern cooking. Its active ingredient, curcumin, has an earthy, slightly bitter, peppery flavour and a mustardy smell. It is a proven anti-fungal, antimicrobial and anti-inflammatory, and widely used to treat wounds in India.

Vanilla is a flavouring derived from the unripe fruits of the only member of the orchid family used in food (Vanilla planifolia). Native to Central America, it was originally used by the Aztecs to flavour their chocolatl, and was brought to Europe by the Spanish and is now mainly grown in Puerto Rico, Madagascar and Réunion. Its sweet mellow perfumed flavour has become almost indispensable in baking, sweet dishes, ice creams and confectionery. However, after saffron, it is one of the most expensive of spices, so many artificial vanilla-like flavourings have been invented. These – usually quite inferior and cloying – may even describe themselves as 'extracts' or 'essences', so look for the word 'pure' and use price as a guide. Better still, buy the whole dried pods. To use them, split them lengthways and scrape out the seeds with a knife. Use the seeds whole or ground, as well as the pod if appropriate, or put the used pods in a jar of sugar to give you a wonderfully flavoured ingredient for sweet sauces and baking.

Wasabi is sometimes called Japanese horseradish and is also made from the root of a plant (Wasabia japonica), though unrelated. The flesh of the root is finely grated our ground and then usually mixed to a paste with water. It is this paste that accompanies sushi and sashimi, mixed with a little soy sauce to accompany the fish.

Worcestershire Sauce has a legendary origin in that a barrel of vinegar and spices made up for a customer to an Indian recipe in the early 1800s was found inedible and left forgotten in the cellar of Worcester chemists, Lea & Perrins. On the point of being thrown out, someone had the wit to taste it, only to find that fermentation had improved it beyond measure and thus was born one of the world's best-known proprietary sauces. Among the identifiable ingredients are garlic, soy sauce, onions, molasses, lime, tamarind and anchovies. Now widely used in kitchens from the Americas to Japan, it has long been the 'secret ingredient' of many home cooks and chefs, providing depth of flavour and umami to all sorts of dishes before even the Japanese had identified the latter. Perhaps its best-known uses are in Bloody Marys and on Welsh rabbit.

My favourite source of herbs, spices and flowers is www.steenbergs.co.uk

Index

Acknowledgements

First published in 2011 by
Quadrille Publishing Limited,
Alhambra House,
27–31 Charing Cross Road,
London WC2H OLS

Editorial Director: Jane O'Shea
Creative Director: Helen Lewis
Editor and project manager: Lewis Esson
Design and art direction: Untitled
Photography: Adam Laycock (except for pages 97, 111, 167 Christopher Scholey and 143 David Hawkins
Food styling: Lesley Sendall with Laura Santtini
Prop styling: Laura Santtini
Production: Vincent Smith, Leonie Kellman

Text © Laura Santtini 2011
Photographs © Adam Laycock 2011 (except for pages 85, 97, 111, 167 © Christopher Scholey)
Illustrations: page 27 'Euphrosyne's Elogium' © Michael Angove; page 57 © Kate Wilson; page 129; Lyn Winter, Green Flash (2011), acrylic on canvas, 8x10 inches, courtesy of the artist

Edited text, design & layout
© Quadrille Publishing Ltd 2011

Cataloguing in Publication Data: a catalogue record for this book is available from the British Library.

ISBN 978 184400 995 4

Printed and bound in China.

Author's Flash Credits

I am so grateful to the following people who have each added their own unique and remarkable flavour to this book. I thank you for helping me achieve a taste of something I could only have dreamt of without your help and support.

My husband, photographer **Christopher Scholey**, whose remarkable eye and thoughts continue to challenge and inspire my writing, in love and in light. **Mathilda and Giacomo** for being wonderfully and independently discerning when it comes to flavours and feelings. **Josie Miguel** without whose loving support nothing would be possible. **Janie Schaffer**, **Lyn Winter** and **Goli Zarbafi** for sisterhood. **Michael Angove**, **Kate Wilson** and **Lyn Winter** for allowing the use of their brilliant art. **Rokelle Lerner** and the **Inner Path Women's Retreat** (class of October 2010) you know who you are! My agent **Caroline Michel** at PFD for making Flash things happen. **Nobu Matsuhisa** for inspiration and collaboration. **Lewis Esson**, my tireless editor and partner in crime, for his sensitive and very clever work. **Jane O'Shea** at Quadrille for her continued belief, and yet again extracting a better book than the one proposed. **Helen Lewis** for giving the project a strong creative blueprint. **Alison Cathie** and the Quadrille sales team, for taking on flavours and feelings. **David Hawkins** at Untitled Studio whose cool eye and head made this book look so fly. **Adam Laycock** for taking such natural and edible photographs hardly ever using his flash. **Richard Learoyd** for introducing Adam and useful, clear, creative thinking. **Lesley Sendall** for being a brilliant and most patient food stylist and friend. **Cristian Gardin**, executive chef at Santini London, for inspiration and help with the cooking. **Tara Walker**, aka The Tasty Tart, for testing each and every recipe and for friendship and support when life was less than flash. **Kim Yorio** – YC Media New York, for strategic thinking and an incredibly flash year. For **Flash UK** & **European Press** and daily support, **Sarah Canet** and **Alice Stanners** at Spoon PR London. **Clare Lattin** and **Mark McGinlay** at Quadrille Publishing for getting the word out.

Important Notes

The author is not a doctor or nutrition specialist and the recommendations and dietary advice provided are based on her personal experience. The advice and recommendations provided may not apply in any individual case and are not intended as a substitute for specialist advice from a doctor or nutrition expert. If you have any concerns or queries in relation to diet or nutrition the author and publishers recommend that you contact a specialist.

The author suggests using edible metals in certain recipes. This is a suggestion and not a recommendation, and the use and consumption of such metals is at your own risk. Neither the author nor the publisher accepts any liability for any illness, harm or injury arising from the use or consumption of such metals. Always read labels, warnings and directions on the packaging of such products before use.

'Flash Cooking' and 'Taste #5 Umami Paste' are trademarks of Laura Santtini